WHEN USING KITCHEN APPLIANCES PLEASE ALWAYS FOLLOW
THE MANUFACTURER'S INSTRUCTIONS

HarperCollins*Publishers*
1 London Bridge Street
London SE1 9GF

www.harpercollins.co.uk

HarperCollins*Publishers*
Macken House, 39/40 Mayor Street Upper
Dublin 1, D01 C9W8, Ireland

First published by HarperCollins*Publishers* 2025

10 9 8 7 6 5 4 3 2 1

© HarperCollins*Publishers* 2025

Heather Thomas asserts the moral right to be identified as the author of this work

A catalogue record of this book is available from the British Library

ISBN 978-0-00-878033-3

Photographer: Andrew Burton
Food Stylist: Pippa Leon
Prop Stylist: Faye Wears

Printed and bound by PNB, Latvia

All rights reserved. No part of this publication may be reproduced, stored in a retrieval system, or transmitted, in any form or by any means, electronic, mechanical, photocopying, recording or otherwise, without the prior written permission of the publishers.

Without limiting the exclusive rights of any author, contributor or the publisher of this publication, any unauthorised use of this publication to train generative artificial intelligence (AI) technologies is expressly prohibited. HarperCollins also exercise their rights under Article 4(3) of the Digital Single Market Directive 2019/790 and expressly reserve this publication from the text and data mining exception.

This book is produced from FSC™ certified paper and other controlled sources to ensure responsible forest management.

For more information visit: www.harpercollins.co.uk/green

THE HAGGIS COOKBOOK

HEATHER THOMAS

HarperCollins*Publishers*

CONTENTS

INTRODUCTION 7

BASIC RECIPES 12

BURNS NIGHT SUPPER 24

APPETIZERS AND STARTERS 34

BRUNCHES AND LIGHT MEALS 44

MAIN MEALS 66

SNACKS AND SANDWICHES 92

INTRODUCTION

Haggis is always the centrepiece of Burns Night supper on 25th January, the birthday of the great Scottish poet Robert Burns. Resting on a silver platter, its arrival is 'piped in' by a lone kilted piper, while the assembled diners perform a slow hand clap. Every year on this night, Scots all over the world gather for a traditional dinner of haggis, neeps (mashed turnips or swede) and tatties (potatoes) served with a 'wee dram' (a glass of Scotch whisky).

Essentially a simple, humble dish born out of hardship and poverty, the haggis was elevated to a national gastronomic treasure in 1787 by Robbie Burns in his famous *Address to a Haggis*, in which he described it as 'the great chieftain of the puddin' race'. This poem is still recited at formal Burns Night celebrations.

WHAT IS HAGGIS?

Contrary to what many people believe, haggis is not 'a wee beastie' running around the heather-covered moorlands of Scotland. It's a savoury, sausage-like 'pudding', which combines minced offal (traditionally sheep's heart, liver and lungs) with oatmeal, onions and spices (usually hot black pepper and grated nutmeg) enclosed in a sausage casing. In the past, this spicy mixture was cooked inside a sheep's stomach, but this is rare nowadays. Suet is sometimes added, too. In spite of its unusual ingredients, the traditional haggis has a pleasantly warm and spicy flavour and, thanks to the inclusion of oats, a distinctive coarse texture, which makes it very appealing.

Luckily, for the squeamish and non-meat eaters (vegetarians and vegans), delicious plant-based alternatives are now available, which you can order online or purchase in many supermarkets and delis. Alternatively, you can make your own at home.

Of course, you don't have to enjoy haggis just once a year on Burns Night. Many people like to serve it on St Andrew's Day, Hogmanay or cold autumnal and winter evenings as well as for breakfast, brunch, snacks and family gatherings. Over the last decade, it has risen to global prominence and it's not an annual one-day event anymore – it tastes great all the year round and is extremely versatile. It's popular not only in English-speaking countries like the United States, Australia, New Zealand and Canada. As the demand continues to grow, Scotland's largest haggis manufacturers are exporting to many more international markets, including Europe, Africa and the Far East. The same goes for sales of vegetarian and vegan haggis, which are becoming very popular, especially during 'Veganuary'.

Note: Haggis is revered by people of Scottish ancestry, particularly in the United States. However, human consumption of sheep's lungs is prohibited there, so Scottish manufacturers are creating new 'compliant' recipes for the US market, substituting sheep's heart for lungs.

THE ORIGINS OF HAGGIS

How and where did haggis originate? Well, the answers to this question are surprising and its actual origins are probably lost in the mists of time. They may even date back to prehistory and ancient Greece. In his epic poem *The Odyssey*, Homer wrote about a man standing 'before a great blazing fire, turning swiftly a stomach full of fat and blood'.

The name provides us with further clues. The word 'haggis' may be derived from the old Scottish word 'hag' (to chop or hew) or from the Swedish 'hagga' or Icelandic 'hogva', which have the same meaning. Indeed, similar dishes to haggis are still eaten today throughout Scandinavia.

Another theory (which is anathema to Scots) is that haggis originated not in Scotland but in England. There are mediaeval references to 'hagws' and a 'puddynge' made from sheep's innards as far back as the 1440s in Norfolk and Lancashire.

It was not until the seventeenth century that haggis was recorded as being eaten in Scotland. Poverty was rife and land enclosures and new farming techniques made offal one of the few foods that many people could afford. By the mid-eighteenth century, the English thought it uncivilised and started to call it, mockingly, 'the Scottish dish', and it was then that Robbie Burns penned his famous *Address to a Haggis*, which is still recited at every Burns Night dinner. And, as they say, the rest is history.

HEALTH AND NUTRITION

The traditional haggis is packed with protein and is a good source of vitamins (A, B12 and folate), essential minerals (iron, zinc and selenium) and dietary fibre. Because it tends to be quite high in fat, it is possible to buy reduced-fat alternatives. Read the labels carefully on commercially produced haggis, as products do vary; for example, some don't contain liver, making them suitable for pregnant women, while others omit sheep's lungs. Indeed, sometimes minced or chopped lean beef or lamb replaces the offal, lowering the fat content and making the flavour more palatable for some people.

Vegetarian and vegan haggis are usually made from a mixture of healthy fresh vegetables, pulses (usually lentils or split peas), grains (pearl barley), oatmeal, seeds and spices, making them highly nutritious and a good source of gut-friendly fibre.

VARIETY AND RECIPES

If you ever thought that haggis is boring, this book will change your mind. We have elegant recipes for snacks, brunches, appetizers, light meals and delicious main courses, as well as the traditional Burns Night feast. We even have ideas for using up leftover haggis.

And if you don't like offal, we offer great veggie and vegan alternatives as well as a reduced-fat version made with minced beef or lamb, oats and spices. Haggis aficionados will also enjoy experimenting with some unusual but tasty dishes, such as haggis sushi, sausage rolls, Chinese dumplings, curries and burritos.

HOW TO COOK HAGGIS

Most people do not prepare and cook haggis themselves as it can be very time-consuming and many people dislike handling offal. Instead, they buy it from their butcher, deli, local supermarket or online. We have provided recipes (see pages 15 and 19) to create your own meaty or plant-based haggis from scratch at home if you want to try it, but the recipes in this book are all suitable for bought alternatives.

All haggis is pre-cooked before being sold, and you should always follow the instructions on the packet or ask your butcher before using. If you are using pre-cooked, packaged haggis in these recipes, it does not need to be heated before being used, unless otherwise stated in the recipe. Haggis is best served piping hot.

Note: You need to remove the outer packaging but not the tight casing and clips before cooking the haggis, unless you are using a microwave.

- **Cooking in water:** the most common way to cook a natural-cased haggis from the butcher is to wrap it in kitchen foil and place it in a large pan of boiling water and then reduce the heat to a gentle simmer. Cook for the recommended time for its size and weight, topping up with water as required so as to keep it covered, and then remove. Before serving, slit open the casing with a knife to release the filling.

- **Oven baking:** alternatively, you can bake a haggis, wrapped in kitchen foil, in a baking dish in a preheated oven at 200°C (180°C fan)/400°F/gas 6 – the cooking time will depend on the size and weight.

- **Cooking in a microwave:** remove the outer packaging and the tight casing and clips from a bought cooked haggis and cut into 1cm (½ inch) slices. Arrange them on a microwaveable plate or dish and cook on Medium, stirring once during cooking, for the recommended time.

- **Cooking in an air fryer:** place the haggis (in its casing) in an air fryer liner and cut a slit across the top of the casing. For a 450g (1lb) haggis, air fry for 10 minutes at 190°C (375°F). Remove the haggis from the air fryer and discard the casing. Mash the haggis with a fork and return to the air fryer for 10 minutes at the same temperature until it is piping hot.

BASIC RECIPES

VARIATIONS
- Add some suet (about 100g/3½oz) to the haggis mixture.
- Make the haggis spicier by adding a good pinch of ground allspice.
- Add a little dried thyme or rosemary.

HOMEMADE TRADITIONAL HAGGIS

This is a traditional haggis recipe and not for the faint-hearted. It is flexible and you can omit the liver or the lungs, if wished, and replace them with minced beef or lamb. You can ask your butcher for some lamb or beef trimmings or use some fatty stewing steak instead. Of course, you don't have to go to all the effort of making your own haggis – you can buy it online or from most delis and supermarkets. However, if you're an aficionado and are up for the challenge, here's how.

SERVES 4
PREP 30 MINUTES
SOAK OVERNIGHT
COOK 4–5 HOURS

1 sheep's stomach or ox (beef) bung
1 lamb's heart, liver and lungs (see note)
450g (1lb) lamb or beef trimmings or stewing steak (lean meat and fat)
1 large onion, diced
225g (8oz/2¾ cups) oatmeal
2 tsp ground coriander seeds
1 tsp freshly grated nutmeg
1 tsp ground mace
1 tbsp fine sea salt
1 tbsp freshly ground black pepper

Tip: Prick the filled stomach bag with a needle before cooking so it doesn't burst in the pan.

NOTE
Lamb's lungs are prohibited in the United States for human consumption.

Clean the sheep's stomach or ox bung, then scald it in boiling water, turn it inside out and soak in a large bowl of cold salted water overnight.

The following day, wash the heart, liver and lungs under running cold water – if wished, place them in a bowl of cold salted water and soak for 2–3 hours, changing the water occasionally.

Drain and place them in a large saucepan together with the lamb or beef trimmings. Cover with cold water and set over a high heat. Bring to the boil, skimming the surface regularly, then reduce the heat to a gentle simmer and cook for 2 hours.

Remove the offal and meat from the pan (keep the liquid) with tongs and rinse in cold water. Transfer to a bowl and set aside to cool before mincing or dicing.

Transfer to a mixing bowl and stir in the onion, oatmeal, spices and seasoning. Pour in a little of the reserved cooking liquid and mix well until the haggis mixture is softened, moist and clings together.

Stuff the mixture into the sheep's stomach, expel any air and close the hole by tying it tightly with some string.

Fill a large saucepan with water – enough to cover the filled haggis – and bring to the boil. Reduce the heat and simmer for 2–3 hours, topping it up regularly to keep it covered. You can test whether it's cooked with a meat thermometer – the internal temperature should be at least 74°C (165°F).

Remove the haggis to a plate and gently cut it open and remove the filling.

HAGGIS SAUSAGES

Most commercial haggis manufacturers sell their own-brand sausages (traditional meaty and vegetarian/vegan), but if you're feeling adventurous, you can make your own using Homemade Tradtional Haggis (see page 15). Sausage casings are available online.

MAKES 8 SAUSAGES
PREP 10 MINUTES
CHILL 12 HOURS OR OVERNIGHT (OPTIONAL)
COOK 10–20 MINUTES

300g (10oz) haggis
150g (5oz) pork sausage meat
sausage casings

Crumble the haggis into a bowl and add the pork sausage meat. Mix them together with a spoon or your hands.

Push the mixture through a sausage stuffing machine (if you have one) fitted with the recommended casings, following the instructions.

Alternatively, divide the mixture into eight equal-sized portions and place each one on a piece of cling film (plastic wrap). Cover with the wrap and tightly roll/mould each one into a sausage shape. Wrap them individually in kitchen foil and chill in the fridge for 12 hours or overnight.

Cook the sausages in an oiled frying pan (skillet) set over a medium heat, turning occasionally, until browned all over and cooked through, about 10–15 minutes. Or place them in an oiled roasting pan and bake in a preheated oven at 190°C (170°C fan)/375°F/ gas 5 for about 20 minutes, until nicely browned and thoroughly cooked.

Tip: You can use the mixture in the first step above to make Sausage Rolls (see page 103).

VEGETARIAN/VEGAN VARIATION
- Take 450g (1lb) Vegetarian/Vegan Haggis mixture before baking (see page 19) and shape into sausages as above. Fry or bake until browned and cooked through.

EASY REDUCED-FAT HAGGIS

If you feel slightly queasy about eating offal (heart, liver and lungs) but want to enjoy some spicy haggis, this recipe is the next best thing to the real deal . . . and it's quicker to prepare and to cook. It is also less fatty than a traditional haggis.

SERVES 4
PREP 10 MINUTES
COOK 1–1¼ HOURS

1 tbsp olive oil
15g (½oz/1 tbsp) unsalted butter
2 onions, diced
1 tsp freshly grated nutmeg
1 tsp ground mace
1 tsp ground coriander
1 tsp freshly ground black pepper
½ tsp ground allspice
leaves stripped from
   3 sprigs of thyme
500g (1lb 2oz) minced (ground)
   beef (max. 5% fat) or lamb
250g (9oz) lamb's liver or
   chicken livers, diced (any fatty
   or hard pieces discarded)
240ml (8fl oz/1 cup) hot
   beef stock
115g (4oz/¾ cup) steel-cut oats
¼ tsp sea salt

TO SERVE:
Gravy (see pages 20–22)
Tatties (see page 27)
Bashed Neeps (see page 27)

Preheat the oven to 180°C (160°C fan)/350°F/gas 4.

Heat the oil and butter in a large pan set over a low to medium heat. Add the onion and cook, stirring occasionally, for about 6–8 minutes, until tender. Stir in the spices and thyme leaves and cook for 2 minutes.

Add the minced meat and liver and cook, stirring occasionally, for 4–5 minutes until browned all over. Stir in the stock, then cover the pan with a lid and simmer gently for 15–20 minutes. Stir in the oats, distributing them throughout the mixture, and season with salt.

Spoon the mixture into a baking dish and level the top. Cover the dish with a lid or some kitchen foil and bake in the preheated oven for 30 minutes. Uncover and cook for 5–10 minutes until appetizingly brown and crisp on top.

Serve immediately with gravy, tatties and bashed neeps or some green vegetables.

VARIATIONS
- You can substitute brown or green lentils for the split peas. Cook until just tender.
- Rolled oats can be used instead of pinhead oatmeal but give a different result and texture.
- The Marmite adds a lovely umami flavour but if it's too salty for you, just use stock.
- Use vegan plant-based butter instead of olive oil.

VEGETARIAN/VEGAN HAGGIS

You don't have to be veggie or vegan to enjoy this delicious non-meat haggis. It's economical and easy to make and tastes delicious. Serve it with traditional mashed swede or turnips (Bashed Neeps, see page 27) and mashed potatoes (Tatties, see page 27) with lashings of Gravy (see pages 20–22) or Whisky Sauce (see page 23).

SERVES 6–8
SOAK 4 HOURS OR OVERNIGHT
PREP 15 MINUTES
COOK 1 HOUR 30 MINUTES

60g (2oz/generous ¼ cup) yellow split peas
60g (2oz/¼ cup) pearl barley
3 tbsp olive oil, plus extra for greasing
1 large onion, diced
1 large carrot, diced
1 large parsnip, peeled and diced
100g (3½oz) chestnut mushrooms, diced
100g (3½oz/generous ½ cup) pinhead oatmeal (steel-cut oats)
½ tsp ground allspice
¼ tsp ground cinnamon
½ tsp freshly ground black pepper
2 tsp Marmite or yeast extract
480ml (16fl oz/2 cups) hot vegetable stock
sea salt

Tips: The haggis will keep in the fridge for up to 3 days and can be reheated in the oven or microwave.

Soak the split peas in cold water for 4 hours or overnight.

Drain and transfer to a saucepan, cover with cold water and bring to the boil. Cook for 30 minutes, or until tender but not too soft. Drain.

Meanwhile, boil the pearl barley according to the instructions on the packet, until it is just tender but retains a little 'bite'.

Heat the olive oil in a large pan set over a medium heat and cook the onion, stirring occasionally, for 5 minutes, until translucent and softened. Stir in the carrot and parsnip and cook for about 5 minutes, or until just tender. Add the mushrooms and cook, stirring, for 5 minutes. Stir in the split peas, oatmeal, ground spices and black pepper.

Stir the Marmite into the hot stock and add most of it to the pan, setting a little aside. Increase the heat and bring to the boil, then reduce the heat to low to medium and simmer gently, stirring occasionally, for 10–15 minutes, until the mixture absorbs the stock and thickens. If it seems too dry, just add some of the reserved stock to slacken it. Stir in the pearl barley and season to taste.

Meanwhile, preheat the oven to 180°C (160°C fan)/350°F/gas 4. Lightly oil a 900g (2lb) loaf tin or pudding basin.

Fill the loaf tin or pudding basin with the haggis mixture and cover with lightly oiled foil or some baking parchment.

Bake in the preheated oven for 30 minutes. Set aside for 5–10 minutes before turning it out and cutting into slices.

MUSHROOM GRAVY

This umami-flavoured gravy is great with haggis and Haggis Sausages (see page 16). To make it vegan-friendly, use olive oil and vegetable stock and add a dash of soy sauce.

MAKES 420ML (14FL OZ/1¾ CUPS)
PREP 10 MINUTES
COOK 30–35 MINUTES

4 tbsp olive oil or meat dripping
1 large onion, diced
1 garlic clove, crushed
300g (10oz) chestnut or Portobello mushrooms, chopped
2 tbsp plain (all-purpose) flour
480ml (16fl oz/2 cups) hot beef, chicken or vegetable stock
1 tbsp balsamic vinegar
sea salt and freshly ground black pepper

Heat the oil or dripping in a frying pan (skillet) set over a medium heat. Cook the onion, stirring occasionally, for 10 minutes, or until softened and golden.

Add the garlic and mushrooms and cook for 5 minutes, stirring occasionally, until tender and golden brown.

Stir in the flour and cook for 2–3 minutes. Pour in the stock, stirring well to absorb the flour, then add the vinegar and cook for 10–15 minutes, giving the gravy an occasional stir, until reduced and the right consistency for your taste.

Check the seasoning and pour into a sauce boat or gravy jug.

VARIATIONS
- Use porcini or wild mushrooms for extra flavour.
- Add a dash of soy sauce or tamari or some mushroom ketchup for extra flavour.
- Stir in some cream or crème fraîche just before serving.
- Add a pinch of sugar.
- Use dried porcini instead of fresh mushrooms and the soaking water instead of stock.

ONION GRAVY

Serve this tasty gravy with the traditional or vegetarian/vegan haggis, bashed neeps and tatties on Burns Night. It's also a good accompaniment for Haggis Sausages (see page 16) or Haggis Toad in the Hole (see page 76). Use vegetable stock for the vegetarian/vegan version. It freezes well in an airtight container for up to 3 months.

MAKES 360ML (12FL OZ/1½ CUPS)
PREP 5 MINUTES
COOK 20–25 MINUTES

3 tbsp olive oil
2 large onions, thinly sliced
1 tbsp plain (all-purpose) flour
300ml (½ pint/1¼ cups) hot beef, chicken or vegetable stock
60ml (2fl oz/¼ cup) balsamic vinegar
sea salt and freshly ground black pepper

Heat the olive oil in a frying pan (skillet) set over a low heat. Add the onions and cook for 15 minutes, stirring occasionally, until really tender and starting to caramelize.

Stir in the flour and cook for 1 minute. Stir in the stock and balsamic vinegar and turn up the heat to high. Bring to the boil, stirring, and then reduce the heat and let the gravy bubble gently for 5 minutes, or until thickened and smooth.

Season to taste with salt and pepper and transfer to a sauce boat or gravy jug.

> **VARIATIONS**
> - Use red onions instead of white.
> - Use red wine vinegar or cider vinegar.
> - Add some crushed garlic.
> - Sweeten with a little redcurrant jelly or cranberry sauce.

WHISKY GRAVY

Add some Scottish flair to your gravy with a wee dram of Scotch whisky. For a vegetarian version, use olive oil and vegetable stock.

MAKES 300ML (½ PINT/1¼ CUPS)
PREP 5 MINUTES
COOK 8–10 MINUTES

2 tbsp olive oil or chicken fat/meat dripping
2 tbsp plain (all-purpose) flour
1 fresh bay leaf
a few sprigs of thyme
3–4 tbsp whisky
400ml (14fl oz/scant 1¾ cups) hot chicken, beef or vegetable stock
sea salt and freshly ground black pepper

Heat the olive oil, chicken fat or meat dripping in a pan set over a low heat and stir in the flour. Cook for 2 minutes, stirring occasionally with a wooden spoon.

Add the bay leaf, thyme and whisky and continue to cook for 2 minutes, stirring.

Gradually add the stock, a little at a time, stirring between each addition until all the stock has been added. Turn up the heat to medium and cook, stirring occasionally, until the gravy thickens and is smooth.

Check the seasoning, remove and discard the herbs, and pour into a gravy boat or jug.

VARIATIONS
- Add a teaspoon of Dijon mustard with the stock.
- Sauté a finely chopped shallot and a crushed garlic clove in the oil or hot fat before adding the flour.
- Whisk in a knob of butter at the end just before serving.

WHISKY SAUCE

This wonderfully creamy and decadent sauce is perfect for serving with cooked haggis, Haggis Wellington (see page 68) and Balmoral Chicken (see page 32). It's also a great accompaniment to a grilled steak. The amount of whisky used may sound like a lot but most of the alcohol evaporates, leaving a distinctive but subtle flavour.

SERVES 4
PREP 5 MINUTES
COOK 20 MINUTES

15g (½oz/1 tbsp) butter
2 shallots, finely chopped
1 garlic clove, crushed
115ml (4fl oz/½ cup) whisky
150ml (5fl oz/scant ¾ cup) hot beef or vegetable stock
150ml (5fl oz/scant ¾ cup) double (heavy) cream
1–2 tsp Dijon or wholegrain mustard
sea salt and freshly ground black pepper

Melt the butter in a pan set over a low to medium heat and add the shallots. Cook, stirring occasionally, for 5 minutes, or until softened. Add the garlic and cook for 2 minutes.

Stir in the whisky and cook for 5 minutes, or until the liquid is absorbed and evaporates. Add the stock together with the cream and mustard.

Reduce the heat and simmer gently, stirring occasionally, for 8–10 minutes, or until the sauce reduces and thickens. Check the seasoning, adding salt and pepper to taste.

Transfer to a jug and serve with haggis.

Tips: Taste the sauce when adding the mustard and be guided by your personal taste.

Vegetarians can substitute vegetable stock for beef stock. And vegans can use a plant-based butter and cashew cream or any store-bought dairy-free oat- or soya-based cream.

VARIATIONS
- If you don't have shallots, use a small onion.
- For a really special occasion, use a single malt whisky. It's worth it!

BURNS NIGHT SUPPER

VARIATIONS
- Cook some sliced carrots with the swede.
- Substitute turnips for the swede.
- Serve with some buttered shredded cabbage or kale.

HAGGIS WITH TATTIES AND NEEPS

Haggis served with tatties and neeps is the centrepiece of the traditional Burns Night supper. It is also served sometimes on New Year's Eve (Hogmanay) before the partying and celebrations begin. A wee dram of whisky is the correct accompaniment rather than a glass of wine. You can easily adapt the recipe for vegetarians and vegans by cooking a vegetarian (vegan-friendly) haggis and substituting dairy-free milk and butter.

SERVES 4
PREP 20 MINUTES
COOK 30–45 MINUTES
+ COOKING THE HAGGIS

500g (1lb 2oz) haggis (traditional or vegetarian)
Gravy (see pages 20–22) or Whisky Sauce (see page 23), to serve

TATTIES:
900g (2lb) potatoes, e.g. Maris Piper, peeled and cut into large chunks
60ml (2fl oz/¼ cup) milk
85g (3oz/⅓ cup) butter
sea salt and ground black pepper

BASHED NEEPS:
1 large swede (rutabaga), peeled and cut into cubes
3–4 tbsp milk
60g (2oz/¼ cup) butter
a pinch of freshly grated nutmeg (optional)
sea salt and ground black pepper

Cook the haggis according to the instructions on the packet (or using the recipes on pages 15 and 19). While the haggis is cooking, make the tatties and bashed neeps.

Make the tatties: put the potatoes in a large saucepan and cover with cold water. Add a pinch of salt and set over a high heat. Bring to the boil and cook for 12–15 minutes, or until they are tender but not mushy. Drain in a colander and set aside for 10 minutes to dry.

Meanwhile, make the bashed neeps: add the swede to a large saucepan and cover with cold water. Add a pinch of salt and set over a high heat. Bring to the boil and cook for 16–18 minutes, or until they are tender and cooked right through. Drain in a colander and set aside for 10 minutes to dry.

For the tatties, heat the milk and butter in a large pan set over a low heat and when the butter melts, add the cooked potatoes and mash until smooth and free of lumps. Season to taste with salt and pepper.

For the bashed neeps, return the cooked swede to the pan and mash coarsely with a potato masher. Add a little milk and the butter – the mixture should be slightly lumpy and not too smooth. Season to taste with salt and pepper and some grated nutmeg (if wished).

Serve the haggis with the tatties and bashed neeps accompanied by some gravy or whisky sauce.

HAGGIS STACKS WITH WHISKY SAUCE

This is a very elegant way of serving haggis, tatties and bashed neeps – perfect for a special Burns Night supper and a great way to impress your guests. It's a bit more fiddly than the traditional method but well worth the extra effort.

SERVES 4
PREP 20 MINUTES
COOK 5–10 MINUTES
+ COOKING THE HAGGIS, BASHED NEEPS AND TATTIES

500g (1lb 2oz) haggis (traditional or vegetarian)
1 quantity Bashed Neeps (see page 27)
1 quantity Tatties (see page 27)
680g (1½lb) kale, destemmed and chopped (optional)
sea salt and freshly ground black pepper
chopped parsley, to garnish
Whisky Sauce, to serve (see page 23)

Note: You will need a large round metal ring (about 7.5cm/3 inches deep) to make the stacks. If you don't have one, you could make smaller stacks (two per serving) or even use a washed-out tin can with both ends removed (with a can opener) to create the desired layers.

Cook the haggis according to the instructions on the packet. Keep warm.

Prepare and cook the bashed neeps and the tatties according to the method described on page 27. Keep warm.

Steam or boil the kale, if using, for 5–10 minutes, draining and pressing out any excess water if boiling. Season with salt and pepper.

Assemble the stacks while the haggis, tatties and bashed neeps are still hot: take a steel ring and place it on a serving plate. Spoon one-quarter of the haggis into the ring, flattening it with the back of a spoon. It should fill one-third of the depth of the ring (2.5cm/1 inch).

Cover with a thin layer of cooked kale (if using) and then add a 2.5cm (1 inch) layer of bashed neeps, pressing down gently with the back of a spoon to level it.

Cover with a layer of tatties to fill the ring, smoothing the top with the back of a spoon.

Very slowly and carefully, remove the ring, sliding it off gently so as to keep the stack with its three colourful layers intact.

Wash and dry the ring and repeat on the remaining three plates. Sprinkle a little chopped parsley on top of each stack and serve immediately while the stacks are still hot with some whisky sauce.

ALTERNATIVE METHOD (you will need four rings)
Cut the cold haggis into thick slices using a ring or tin to cut them to the right shape and size. Place the haggis-filled rings on a baking tray (sheet pan) and layer up with the kale, bashed neeps and tatties as described above. Cook in a preheated oven at 190°C (170°C fan)/375°F/gas 5 for 20 minutes. To serve, slide the thin blade of a knife around the inside of each ring and gently lift it off. Use a large slice to transfer the stacks to the serving plates.

HAGGIS BUBBLE AND SQUEAK PATTIES

These crispy patties are a great way of using up any leftovers from your Burns Night supper. Serve them for an easy light lunch or supper or prepare them the evening before and chill in the fridge overnight ready to fry for breakfast or brunch with some poached or fried eggs. Delicious!

SERVES 4
PREP 15 MINUTES
COOK 20 MINUTES

4 tbsp olive oil
2 onions, finely chopped
3 garlic cloves, crushed
500g (1lb 2oz) leftover cooked Tatties (see page 27) and Bashed Neeps (see page 27)
200g (7oz) leftover cooked Brussels sprouts or green cabbage, roughly chopped
200g (7oz) leftover cooked haggis
plain (all-purpose) flour, for dusting
sea salt and freshly ground black pepper
cranberry sauce or relish, to serve

Heat 2 tablespoons of oil in a large frying pan (skillet) set over a medium heat. Cook the onions and garlic, stirring occasionally, for 8–10 minutes or until softened and golden.

Add the cooked tatties, bashed neeps and sprouts or cabbage to the pan and stir well. Crumble in the haggis and stir to distribute it evenly throughout the mixture. Season lightly with salt and pepper.

Transfer to a bowl and when the mixture is cool enough to handle, divide it into eight small or four large portions. Using your hands, mould each one into a patty (burger) and dust lightly with flour.

Heat the remaining oil in a large non-stick frying pan set over a medium heat and cook the burgers for 4–5 minutes each side, or until heated right through and crisp and golden brown. Serve hot with some cranberry sauce or relish.

VARIATIONS
- Spice it up by adding some ground cumin, turmeric and garam masala.
- Cook some grated fresh root ginger with the onions and garlic.

HAGGIS HASH AND EGGS

Nothing gets wasted in this tasty, colourful hash. It's the perfect way to recycle your leftover vegetables and haggis into a quick and easy brunch or family meal.

SERVES 4
PREP 10 MINUTES
COOK 20 MINUTES

2 tbsp olive oil
2 garlic cloves, crushed
½ tsp paprika
450g (1lb) leftover roast potatoes, parsnips, carrots or swede (rutabaga), cubed
400g (14oz) leftover cooked haggis
a small handful of flat-leaf parsley, chopped
4 medium free-range eggs
½ tsp crushed red chilli flakes
sea salt and freshly ground black pepper

Heat the olive oil in a large frying pan (skillet) set over a low to medium heat. Add the garlic and cook for 1 minute without browning. Stir in the paprika and cook for 1 minute.

Add the leftover vegetables and cook for 10 minutes, stirring occasionally, or until tender and starting to colour and crisp. Season to taste with salt and pepper and crumble in the haggis. Cook for 4–5 minutes, stirring occasionally, and then stir in the parsley.

Meanwhile, break the eggs into a saucepan of simmering water and poach for 3–4 minutes or until the whites are set and the yolks are still runny. Remove carefully with a slotted spoon and drain on kitchen paper (paper towels).

Divide the hash among four serving plates and top each one with a poached egg sprinkled with chilli flakes. Serve immediately.

VARIATIONS
- Add some fried onions or leeks.
- Add some cherry or baby plum tomatoes.
- Add some leftover cooked peas or shredded greens.
- Fry the eggs instead of poaching them.

BALMORAL CHICKEN

This delicious dish of chicken stuffed with haggis derives its name from Balmoral Castle in the Highlands, the Scottish holiday home of the British Royal Family. The chicken is usually served in a whisky sauce, but we have created one with mushrooms and Marsala to complement the spiciness of the haggis.

SERVES 4
PREP 15 MINUTES
COOK 30-35 MINUTES

olive oil, for brushing
4 large chicken breasts, skinned
175g (6oz) haggis
8 slices of streaky bacon or pancetta, rind removed
Tatties (see page 27) or boiled potatoes, to serve
broccoli or green beans, to serve

MUSHROOM SAUCE:
2 tbsp olive oil
15g (½ oz/1 tbsp) butter
250g (9oz) chestnut mushrooms, thinly sliced
240ml (8fl oz/1 cup) Marsala
3–4 tbsp crème fraîche
a few sprigs of parsley, finely chopped
sea salt and freshly ground black pepper

> **VARIATIONS**
> - Serve with Whisky Sauce (see page 23).
> - If you don't have Marsala, use Madeira instead.

Preheat the oven to 180°C (160°C fan)/350°F/gas 4. Lightly brush a baking dish with olive oil.

With a sharp knife, cut a slit along one side of each chicken breast. Insert the knife into the slit to create a deep pocket inside the breast without cutting through the other side.

Divide the haggis into four portions and use to fill the pockets, pushing it in deeply.

Using the blade of the knife, stretch out the bacon slices to make them thinner and longer. Wrap two slices around each chicken breast with the ends underneath.

Place the bacon-wrapped chicken in the oiled baking dish and cook in the preheated oven for 30–35 minutes, or until the chicken is golden brown and cooked right through and the bacon is crisp.

While the chicken is cooking, make the mushroom sauce: heat the oil and butter in a large frying pan (skillet) set over a medium heat and cook the mushrooms for 5 minutes or until tender and golden brown. Add the Marsala to the pan and increase the heat. When it's bubbling and starting to reduce, turn down the heat to a gentle simmer and cook gently for 10–15 minutes or until the sauce has reduced and thickened. If it's too thick, you can thin it with a little chicken stock. Season to taste with salt and pepper and stir in the crème fraîche and parsley.

Serve the chicken breasts in a pool of mushroom sauce with tatties or boiled potatoes and some green vegetables.

APPETIZERS AND STARTERS

STEAMED CHINESE HAGGIS DUMPLINGS

These delicious little dumplings are quick and easy and a great way of introducing people to haggis or using up the leftovers. You can buy ready-made dumpling wrappers in some supermarkets or online.

SERVES 4
PREP 35 MINUTES
COOK 8–10 MINUTES

125g (4½oz) haggis, crumbled
75g (3oz) chopped napa (Chinese) cabbage or pak choi
2 spring onions (scallions), diced
2.5cm (1 inch) piece of fresh root ginger, peeled and grated
1 tbsp soy sauce
1 tsp sesame oil
a pinch of caster (superfine) sugar
2 tbsp light olive oil, for frying
salt and ground black pepper

DIPPING SAUCE:
2 tbsp rice vinegar
1 tbsp dark soy sauce
1 tsp toasted sesame oil
1 tsp caster (superfine) sugar
½ tsp grated fresh root ginger
1 small red chilli, diced
juice of ½ lime
2 spring onions (scallions), sliced

DUMPLING WRAPPERS:
150g (5oz/scant 1½ cups) plain (all-purpose) flour, plus extra for dusting
120ml (4fl oz/½ cup) very hot water

Make the dipping sauce: mix all the ingredients together in a bowl and set aside.

Make the dumpling wrappers: put the flour in a large bowl and gradually stir in the hot water, mixing it with a fork, until you have a ball of dough. If it's a bit dry, add a little more water.

Using your hands, knead the dough on a lightly floured work surface until it's smooth – it will take 6–8 minutes. Put in a bowl, cover with a clean damp cloth and set aside for 15 minutes.

Meanwhile, mix the haggis, cabbage, spring onions, ginger, soy sauce, sesame oil and sugar in a bowl, and season lightly.

Knead the dough for 5 minutes until smooth and elastic. Mould it into a long cylinder, 2.5cm (1 inch) diameter, and cut it into 12 pieces. Use a rolling pin to flatten each piece and roll it out into a thin circle about 10cm (4 inches) wide. Cover the dough circles with a damp cloth to stop them drying out as you work.

Divide the filling among the dough circles, placing a little pile in the middle of each one. Brush the edge of each circle with water and fold the dough over the top of the filling to make a semicircle. Pleat round the edge, pinching the dough with your fingers to seal it.

Set a large non-stick frying pan (skillet) with a lid over a medium to high heat. Pour in the oil and when it's hot, add the dumplings. Cook for 2–3 minutes, or until they are crispy and brown underneath. Pour in 5 tablespoons water and cover the pan with a tight-fitting lid. Steam for 5 minutes, or until the liquid has been absorbed. Uncover the pan and cook for 1–2 minutes to crisp the bottoms of the dumplings.

Serve immediately with the dipping sauce.

VARIATIONS
- Drizzle the dumplings with chilli oil.
- Add some crushed garlic to the haggis filling or dipping sauce.

V HAGGIS CROQUETTES WITH TOMATO CHILLI JAM

For people who are unfamiliar with haggis or nervous about trying it, these tasty croquettes are the perfect introduction. If you are serving with tomato chilli jam, you will have to make it in advance. It will keep for up to 12 months stored in a cool, dry place. Once opened, keep it in the fridge.

MAKES 20 CROQUETTES
CHILLI JAM: PREP 15 MINUTES
  COOK 1 HOUR
CROQUETTES: PREP 40 MINUTES
  COOK 10–15 MINUTES

450g (1lb) potatoes, peeled
85g (3oz/¾ cup) grated mature Cheddar cheese
2 small free-range eggs, beaten
2 tbsp plain (all-purpose) flour, plus extra for dusting
175g (6oz) vegetarian haggis, crumbled
a few sprigs of parsley, finely chopped
vegetable oil, for deep-frying
sea salt and black pepper

TOMATO CHILLI JAM:
1kg (2lb 3oz) ripe tomatoes
4 garlic cloves, peeled
5cm (2 inch) piece of fresh root ginger, peeled and chopped
3–4 large red chillies, stemmed and halved
3 tbsp soy sauce
600g (1lb 5oz/2½ cups) granulated sugar
240ml (8fl oz/1 cup) red wine vinegar or cider vinegar

Make the tomato chilli jam: blitz half the tomatoes in a food processor with the garlic, ginger, chillies and soy sauce. Transfer to a large heavy-based saucepan and add the sugar and vinegar. Stir over a low to medium heat until the sugar dissolves and then bring to the boil.

Meanwhile, chop the remaining tomatoes and add to the boiling mixture. Reduce the heat and simmer for 45 minutes, stirring, until the mixture reduces and thickens (don't worry if it takes longer).

Pour into sterilized jars, cover with waxed paper discs and lids, and store in a cool, dry place.

Cut the potatoes into quarters and cook in a pan of boiling salted water for 25 minutes, or until tender but not mushy. Drain well and pass through a potato ricer or mash with a potato masher.

Add the grated Cheddar, beaten eggs and flour and mix well until everything is thoroughly incorporated. Mix in the haggis and parsley, distributing them evenly throughout the mixture, and season with salt and pepper. Set aside to cool.

When the mixture is cool, divide into 20 equal-sized pieces and shape each one into a small cylinder. Place them on a baking tray (sheet pan) and lightly dust with flour.

Heat the oil in a deep fryer, large heavy saucepan or a deep frying pan (skillet) and when it's hot (170°C/340°F) start adding the croquettes, three or four at a time. Fry for 2 minutes, or until golden brown all over. Remove from the pan with a slotted spoon and drain on kitchen paper (paper towels). Serve piping hot with the tomato chilli jam.

FESTIVE CHEESY HAGGIS BITES

These bite-sized cheesy treats are perfect for festive parties, a Christmas appetizer or pre-Burns Night dinner canapés. They are wonderfully easy to make and you can prepare them in advance and pop them into the oven as your guests arrive to serve hot with drinks. We've used vegetarian haggis but the traditional sort tastes just as good.

MAKES 24 BITES
PREP 15 MINUTES
COOK 12–15 MINUTES

spray olive oil
plain (all-purpose) flour, for dusting
1 sheet of frozen puff pastry, thawed
200g (7oz) firm unripe Brie, straight from the fridge
200g (7oz) vegetarian haggis, crumbled
24 tsp cranberry sauce
24 mini sprigs of rosemary

Preheat the oven to 200°C (180°C fan)/400°F/gas 6. Lightly spray a non-stick 24-cup mini muffin pan with oil.

Lightly dust a clean work surface with flour and roll the puff pastry sheet into a 37 x 25cm (15 x 10 inch) rectangle and cut into 24 equal-sized squares.

Place a square in each mini muffin cup, pressing it all the way in to fill the hole and letting the edges rise at the sides.

Cut the cold Brie into 24 small pieces (don't remove the rind) and place one in each muffin cup. Crumble in the haggis and then top with the cranberry sauce.

Bake in the preheated oven for 12–15 minutes, or until the pastry is puffy, crisp and golden brown and the cheese has melted.

Garnish with rosemary sprigs and serve. Delicious!

VARIATIONS
- Use little tartlets or filo (phyllo) pastry instead of puff pastry.
- Sprinkle with snipped chives.
- Substitute Camembert or goat's cheese for the Brie.

APPETIZERS AND STARTERS

HAGGIS PIGS IN BLANKETS

If you love crispy bacon-wrapped sausages, enjoy them the Scottish way and use gently spiced haggis sausage meat instead. North of the border, they are often referred to as 'kilted' sausages. You can eat them all year round as appetizers, party canapés or as the perfect accompaniment to roast chicken.

MAKES ABOUT 16 PIGS IN BLANKETS
PREP 20 MINUTES
COOK 15–20 MINUTES

450g (1lb) Haggis Sausages meat (see page 16)
4 sage leaves, finely chopped
leaves stripped from 3 sprigs of thyme
2 spring onions (scallions) tops, diced
16 thin slices of streaky bacon or pancetta
cranberry sauce, to serve

Preheat the oven to 190°C (170°C fan)/375°F/gas 5.

Put the haggis sausage meat in a bowl with the herbs and spring onion tops. Stir well to distribute them evenly throughout the mixture.

Spoon the mixture into a piping bag and cut a chipolata-sized (diameter) hole at the end of the bag. Pipe 16 thin sausages (about 7.5cm/3 inches long) on to a sheet of non-stick baking parchment.

Wrap a thin slice of bacon or pancetta around each sausage and place on a non-stick baking tray (sheet pan).

Cook in the preheated oven for 15–20 minutes, or until the sausages are cooked, appetizingly browned and the bacon/pancetta is golden and crisp. Serve hot with cranberry sauce.

> **VARIATIONS**
> - Drizzle the cooked sausages with a little honey and pop them back in the oven for 3–4 minutes.
> - Alternatively, you can shape the mixture into balls instead of sausages before wrapping them in bacon or pancetta. Cook in the oven in the same way.

CREAMY HAGGIS SOUP

A comforting and delicious bowl of soup for a cold winter's day. This soup freezes well so you could make double the quantity and freeze a batch for Burns Night supper.

SERVES 4
PREP 15 MINUTES
COOK 40 MINUTES

1 tbsp olive oil
15g (½oz/1 tbsp) butter
1 onion, chopped
1 leek, cleaned, trimmed and chopped
2 celery sticks, chopped
1 large carrot, chopped
250g (9oz) swede (rutabaga), peeled and diced
2 potatoes, peeled and diced
600ml (21fl oz/2½ cups) hot chicken or vegetable stock
200ml (7fl oz/scant 1 cup) milk
½ tsp ground nutmeg
a pinch of sweet paprika
115g (4oz) haggis, crumbled
a few sprigs of parsley, chopped
sea salt and freshly ground black pepper

Heat the olive oil and butter in a saucepan set over a medium heat. Add the onion, leek, celery and carrot, and cook, stirring occasionally, for 6–8 minutes, or until softened.

Stir in the swede and potatoes and cook for 3–4 minutes. Add the stock and bring to the boil. Reduce the heat and simmer for 20 minutes or until all the vegetables are tender.

Transfer to a food processor or blender and blitz until smooth, then return to the pan. Alternatively, you can use a stick blender.

Stir in the milk, nutmeg and paprika, and reheat gently over a low heat. Check the seasoning, adding salt and pepper to taste if needed.

Put the haggis in a frying pan (skillet) set over a medium heat and stir gently until it's really hot.

Divide the soup among four bowls and sprinkle with parsley. Crumble the haggis over the top and serve.

Tip: If you're in a hurry, cook the haggis in the microwave before crumbling it into the soup.

VARIATIONS
- Spice up the soup with a pinch of ground cinnamon, cumin and/or coriander.
- Swirl a spoonful of crème fraîche into each bowl, just before garnishing and serving.

HAGGIS SUSHI

Sushi is really healthy and the good news is that you can make it with haggis! It's surprisingly quick and easy to prepare and tastes delicious. Try it and see for yourself.

SERVES 4
PREP 25 MINUTES
COOK 10–15 MINUTES

300g (10oz/1¼ cups) sushi rice
2 tbsp rice vinegar
1 tsp mirin
1 tsp black sesame seeds, plus extra for sprinkling
1 tsp caster (superfine) sugar
1 carrot
2 tsp soy sauce
¼ cucumber, peeled, deseeded and cut into very thin strips lengthways
4 sheets of nori seaweed
200g (7oz) vegetarian haggis
vegetarian teriyaki or soy sauce, pickled ginger and wasabi, to serve (optional)

Cook the rice according to the directions on the packet – it will take 10–15 minutes until it's tender and all the water has been absorbed. Stir in the vinegar, mirin, sesame seeds and sugar, then cover the pan and leave to cool until the rice is at room temperature.

Cut the carrot into thin julienne strips and blanch in a pan of boiling water for 1 minute. Remove and plunge into cold water. When cool, sprinkle with 1 teaspoon of the soy sauce. Sprinkle the cucumber with the remaining soy sauce.

Place a nori sheet, shiny-side down, on a bamboo sushi mat or work surface covered with cling film (plastic wrap). Spread the cooled rice over the sheet, leaving a 1cm (½ inch) border along the long edge.

Crumble the haggis over the rice and then lay the carrot and cucumber strips on top.

Using the cling film and sushi mat (if applicable), lift the long bottom edge over the filling and roll up firmly towards the top, pressing down as you do so. When you reach the top, moisten the edge of the nori with water to seal. Repeat with the remaining sheets to make four rolls. If wished, wrap the rolls in cling film in the fridge until ready to serve.

Cut each roll into eight rounds and serve, sprinkled with sesame seeds, with teriyaki or soy sauce, pickled ginger and wasabi for sprinkling or dipping.

VARIATIONS
- Add some diced avocado to the filling.
- Add some long fresh chives.

APPETIZERS AND STARTERS

BRUNCHES AND LIGHT MEALS

EASY HAGGIS AND MUSHROOM PLAIT

A crisp, golden puff pastry plaited (braided) pie looks impressive but is actually very easy to make. Vegans can use vegan puff pastry, omit the butter and glaze the pie with aquafaba (canned chickpea/garbanzo liquid) or nut milk before baking.

SERVES 4–6
PREP 20 MINUTES
COOK 45–55 MINUTES

2 tbsp olive oil, plus extra for drizzling
2 red onions, thinly sliced
2 garlic cloves, crushed
15g (½oz/1 tbsp) butter
400g (14oz) white or chestnut mushrooms, sliced
1 x 375g (13oz) pack of ready-rolled puff pastry
plain (all-purpose) flour, for dusting
400g (14oz) vegetarian haggis
1 medium free-range egg, beaten
sesame seeds and nigella (black onion) seeds, for sprinkling
sea salt and freshly ground black pepper

Preheat the oven to 200°C (180°C fan)/400°F/gas 6. Line a baking tray (sheet pan) with baking parchment.

Heat the oil in a large frying pan (skillet) set over a low to medium heat and cook the onion and garlic, stirring occasionally, for 8–10 minutes, or until tender.

Add the butter and the mushrooms and cook, turning occasionally, for 5 minutes, or until tender and golden brown.

Roll out the pastry on a lightly floured surface to a large rectangle – it should be about 3mm (⅛ inch) thick. Place on the lined baking tray and spoon the mushroom mixture lengthways down the centre of the pastry. Put the vegetarian haggis on top.

Cut the pastry diagonally at 2cm (¾ inch) intervals all the way down on both sides from the filling to the edge. Fold the pastry ends over the filling and then raise the strips, alternating from side to side, up and over the filling like a plait (braid). Lightly brush the pastry with beaten egg.

Bake in the preheated oven for 30–40 minutes, or until the pastry is puffed up, golden brown and crisp. Serve cut into slices.

> **VARIATIONS**
> • Add some baby spinach leaves or herbs, e.g. parsley and thyme.
> • Cook a thinly sliced leek with the onions and garlic.

HAGGIS PORTOBELLO MUSHROOMS WITH CHÈVRE

Portobello mushrooms are extra large and thick with a 'meaty' texture – perfect for stuffing and baking. Enjoy them as a light lunch or a delicious Burns Night appetizer.

SERVES 4
PREP 10 MINUTES
COOK 20–25 MINUTES

2 tsp olive oil, plus extra for oiling and drizzling
4 Portobello mushrooms (or large field mushrooms)
2 garlic cloves, crushed
a few sprigs of parsley, chopped
300g (10oz) vegetarian haggis
4 x 25g (1oz) slices of chilled chèvre goat's cheese
sea salt and fresh ground black pepper
red onion chutney or pomegranate molasses, to serve

Preheat the oven to 200°C (180°C fan)/400°F/gas 6. Lightly oil a large baking tray (sheet pan).

Remove the stalks from the mushrooms and chop them. Place the mushrooms, stalk-side up, on the baking tray. Drizzle with olive oil and bake in the preheated oven for 10 minutes.

Meanwhile, heat the olive oil in a small frying pan (skillet) and cook the mushroom stalks and garlic for 4–5 minutes, or until tender and golden. Stir in the parsley and crumble in the cooked haggis. Season to taste with salt and pepper.

Spoon into the mushroom caps and top each one with a slice of chevre. Bake in the oven for 10–15 minutes, or until the mushrooms are cooked and tender and the chevre is softened and golden brown.

Serve immediately with a dollop of red onion chutney.

Tip: Chill the goat's cheese in the fridge before using. It will make it firmer and easier to slice.

VARIATIONS
- Use butter instead of olive oil.
- Add some pine nuts or chopped walnuts to the garlic and mushroom stalk mixture.
- Add some chopped spinach.
- If you don't like goat's cheese, sprinkle with breadcrumbs and grated cheese before baking.

STICKY HAGGIS HOTDOGS

These haggis sausages are deliciously sweet, aromatic and sticky – much more flavourful than the usual frankfurters. They are perfect for serving at Burns Night or bonfire parties, a casual family get together and Halloween. If you don't want to make the sausages yourself, you can use ready-made ones, which are available in some supermarkets and online. Vegetarian Haggis Sausages (see page 16) also work well.

SERVES 4
PREP 10 MINUTES
COOK 20 MINUTES

spray oil
8 Haggis Sausages (see page 16)
2 red onions, thinly sliced
1 tsp nigella (black onion) seeds
1 tbsp balsamic vinegar
4 sub rolls or hot dog rolls
4 tbsp tomato ketchup
sea salt and freshly ground black pepper

STICKY GLAZE:
2 tbsp clear honey
1 tbsp tomato ketchup
1 tbsp balsamic vinegar
1 tsp Dijon mustard

Preheat the oven to 200°C (180°C fan)/400°F/gas 6.

Lightly spray a roasting pan with oil and pop it into the hot oven for 5 minutes to warm it up. Place the sausages in the hot pan and cook for 5 minutes until browned underneath.

Turn them over and add the onions and mustard seeds to the pan. Sprinkle the onions with the balsamic vinegar and season with salt and pepper. Return to the oven for 5 minutes, turning the sausages once.

Mix together the ingredients for the sticky glaze and brush over the sausages. Cook in the oven for a further 10 minutes, or until the sausages are browned, sticky and cooked right through, and the onions are golden and tender.

Split and lightly toast the bread rolls or warm them in a griddle pan. Spread the base of each roll with ketchup and cover with the sausages and onions. Top with the other half of the roll and eat immediately.

VARIATIONS
- Use the sausages and onions for filling split pitta breads or wraps.
- Serve with hot mustard or some fruity relish or chutney.

CHEESY LEEK AND NEEPS HAGGIS TART

This looks a bit of a faff to make, but you can cheat and use ready-made rolled shortcrust pastry (pie crust) if you're in a hurry. And it tastes as good as it looks – eat it hot, lukewarm or at room temperature.

SERVES 6
PREP 20 MINUTES
CHILL 30 MINUTES
COOK 1 HOUR
+ COOKING THE HAGGIS

450g (1lb) swede (rutabaga), peeled and cubed
2 tbsp olive oil, plus extra for drizzling
300g (10oz) vegetarian haggis
1 onion, thinly sliced
2 leeks, cleaned, trimmed and coarsely shredded
2 garlic cloves, crushed
4 medium free-range eggs
300ml (½ pint/1¼ cups) double (heavy) cream
a large pinch of grated nutmeg
100g (3½oz/1 cup) grated cheese
sea salt and freshly ground black pepper

SHORTCRUST PASTRY:
250g (9oz/scant 2½ cups) plain (all-purpose) flour, plus extra for dusting
a pinch of salt
115g (4oz/½ cup) butter, chilled and diced, plus extra for greasing

Make the pastry: sift the flour and salt into a mixing bowl. Add the butter and, using your fingers, rub it into the flour until the mixture resembles breadcrumbs. Stir in 3–4 tablespoons of water, a little at a time, until everything binds together and you have a smooth ball of dough. Wrap it in cling film (plastic wrap) and chill in the fridge for at least 30 minutes.

Meanwhile, preheat the oven to 190°C (170°C fan)/375°F/gas 5. Lightly butter a deep 23cm (9 inch) fluted tart tin.

Place the swede on a baking tray (sheet pan). Drizzle with oil and season. Roast for 20 minutes, or until tender but not mushy.

Cook the haggis according to the packet instructions.

Heat the oil in a frying pan (skillet) set over a low heat and cook the onion, leek and garlic, stirring occasionally, for 15 minutes, or until soft, golden and starting to caramelize.

Beat the eggs in a bowl with the cream. Stir in the nutmeg and season with salt and pepper.

Roll out the pastry on a lightly floured surface and use to line the tart tin. Prick the base lightly with a fork and line with crumpled baking parchment. Fill with baking beans and bake 'blind' for 15 minutes. Remove the paper and baking beans and cool a little.

Cover the base of the tart with the onion and leek mixture and sprinkle the haggis over the top. Gently crush the swede (not too much) and add to the tart with the grated cheese. Pour the beaten egg mixture over the top.

Bake for 25–30 minutes, or until the filling is set and golden brown. Let the tart cool a little before slicing.

VARIATIONS
- Use pumpkin or squash instead of swede.
- Add some fresh baby spinach leaves or watercress.
- This also works well with traditional meat haggis.

VEGGIE HAGGIS BANH MI

These sweet, sour and salty baguettes take longer to prepare and make than the average sandwich, but they're so delicious that it's well worth the effort.

SERVES 2
PREP 20 MINUTES
MARINATE 1 HOUR
COOK 15 MINUTES

1 carrot, cut into thin matchsticks
2 large radishes, thinly sliced
½ red or yellow (bell) pepper, deseeded and thinly sliced
½ small ridged (Lebanese) cucumber, cut into matchsticks
2 tbsp rice vinegar
2 tbsp caster (superfine) sugar
2 tsp vegetarian nam pla (Thai fish sauce)
2 small baguettes (French sticks)
¼ red onion, thinly sliced
lime wedges, for squeezing

CHILLI HAGGIS:
1 tbsp olive oil
1 small onion, finely chopped
2 garlic cloves, crushed
225g (8oz) vegetarian haggis
½ tsp chilli powder
3–4 tbsp hot vegetable stock
1 tbsp sweet chilli sauce
a few sprigs of coriander (cilantro), finely chopped

SPICY MAYO:
60g (2oz/¼ cup) mayonnaise
2 spring onions (scallions), thinly sliced
1–2 tbsp sweet chilli sauce
sea salt crystals

Make the spicy mayo: mix all the ingredients together, seasoning to taste with salt. Cover and chill in the fridge until you're ready to assemble the baguettes.

Mix together the carrot, radishes, red pepper and cucumber in a glass bowl. Heat the vinegar and sugar in a small pan set over a low heat, stirring until the sugar dissolves, then bring to the boil and remove from the heat. Stir in the nam pla and pour over the vegetables. Leave to marinate for at least 1 hour.

When you're ready to eat, make the chilli haggis: heat the oil in a frying pan (skillet) set over a low to medium heat. Cook the onion and garlic for 5 minutes, until starting to soften, and then crumble in the haggis and add the chilli powder and vegetable stock. Cook for 10 minutes. Stir in the sweet chilli sauce and coriander.

Split the baguettes in half lengthways and scoop out most of the soft bread in the centre to leave a crusty shell. Spread the spicy mayo over the bases and add the chilli haggis. Top with the pickled carrot and radish mixture and the onion. Cover with the baguette tops. Serve immediately, while the haggis is still warm, with lime wedges for squeezing.

Tip: Alternatively, you can wrap the assembled baguettes in foil and eat them later as a packed lunch.

CHEESY HAGGIS, MUSHROOM AND SPINACH QUESADILLAS

Quesadillas are very versatile and make a great light lunch served with salad or griddled vegetables. Crisp and golden on the outside and oozing with melted cheese, they are sure to be a hit! They are also a great way of using up leftover cooked haggis.

SERVES 2–4
PREP 10 MINUTES
COOK 15–20 MINUTES

3 tbsp olive oil
300g (10oz) chestnut mushrooms, sliced
115g (4oz) spinach leaves, washed, trimmed and shredded
100g (3½oz/1 cup) grated Cheddar or Monterey Jack cheese
200g (7oz) vegetarian haggis, crumbled
2 spring onions (scallions), thinly sliced
1 hot red chilli, diced
4 large flour or corn tortillas
hot tomato salsa and soured cream, to serve

SMASHED AVOCADO:
1 large ripe avocado, peeled and stoned (pitted)
1 garlic clove, crushed
a pinch of crushed chilli flakes
juice of ½ lime
a few drops of olive oil
sea salt flakes and freshly ground black pepper

Make the smashed avocado: put everything in a bowl and mash coarsely with a fork until well combined but still slightly lumpy and not too smooth. Set aside.

Heat 2 tablespoons of the oil in a large non-stick frying pan (skillet) set over a medium heat and, when it's hot, add the mushrooms and cook, stirring occasionally, for 5 minutes or until they are tender and any water they have released has evaporated. Add the spinach and cook, stirring, for 1–2 minutes – just long enough for it to wilt.

Transfer to a bowl and mix with the grated cheese, crumbled haggis, spring onions and chilli. Stir well and season to taste with salt and pepper.

Spread one-quarter of the mixture over half of one tortilla but not right up to the edge. Fold the other half of the tortilla over the top of the filling and press the edges firmly together to seal them. Repeat with the other tortillas and the rest of the filling.

Heat the remaining oil in a clean large frying pan set over a medium heat and when it's very hot, carefully add two tortillas. Cook for 2–3 minutes, or until golden and crisp underneath.

Use a slice (spatula) to flip them over and cook the other side. They're ready when the filling is hot and the cheese has melted.

Slide the tortillas out of the pan onto a board and cook the remaining tortillas in the same way.

Cut each quesadilla into wedges. Sprinkle with sea salt and serve immediately with the smashed avocado, some salsa and soured cream.

HAGGIS KOFTA KEBABS

Koftas are very versatile and you can spice them up according to your personal taste. They are equally good for an informal Burns Night get-together or a summer barbecue.

SERVES 4
PREP 10 MINUTES
CHILL 30 MINUTES
COOK 10 MINUTES

300g (10oz) haggis, crumbled
200g (7oz) lean minced (ground) lamb
1 small red onion, grated
2 garlic cloves, crushed
1 red chilli, diced
1 tsp ground cumin
1 tsp ground coriander
½ tsp ground cinnamon
a handful of coriander (cilantro), chopped
olive oil, for spraying or brushing
sea salt and freshly ground black pepper

TO SERVE:
boiled rice, couscous or quinoa
chilled yoghurt or tzatziki (see page 59)
tomato and cucumber salad
lemon wedges, for squeezing

Put the haggis and lamb in a bowl with the onion, garlic, chilli, ground spices and coriander. Season with salt and pepper and mix well. Divide the mixture into four equal portions and, using your hands, mould the mixture into four large sausage shapes.

Thread each one onto a metal or pre-soaked wooden skewer and spray or brush lightly with oil. Alternatively, you can mould the mixture into eight smaller sausage shapes and thread two onto each skewer.

Put the koftas onto a lined baking tray (sheet pan) or into a container and chill in the refrigerator for 30 minutes to firm them up before cooking.

Heat a large griddle pan set over a medium heat (or fire up the barbecue) and brush lightly with oil. Add the skewers and cook, turning them frequently, for 10 minutes, or until browned all over and cooked right through. Alternatively, you could cook them under a preheated hot overhead grill (broiler).

Serve hot with rice, couscous or quinoa, a bowl of yoghurt or tzatziki and a chunky tomato and cucumber salad. Squeeze the juice of the lemons over the koftas.

VARIATIONS
- Use minced beef instead of lamb.
- Serve with hummus and warm flatbreads.
- Vary the spices: add some sweet or smoked paprika.

VEGGIE HAGGIS, NEEPS AND SPINACH FRITTATA

A frittata is always a good idea. This one is made with vegetarian haggis and packed with healthy and colourful vegetables. It's so simple to make and perfect for brunch or a light lunch or supper.

SERVES 4
PREP 15 MINUTES
COOK 25–30 MINUTES

300g (10oz) swede (rutabaga), peeled and cubed
1 tbsp olive oil
1 onion, chopped
1 red (bell) pepper, deseeded and chopped
2 garlic cloves, crushed
300g (10oz) vegetarian haggis
100g (3½oz) spinach, shredded
6 large free-range eggs
2 tbsp grated Parmesan or Cheddar cheese
sea salt and freshly ground black pepper

Cook the swede in a saucepan of boiling water for 5–10 minutes until it's just tender but still holds its shape. Drain well.

Meanwhile, heat the oil in a large non-stick frying pan (skillet) set over a low to medium heat and cook the onion, red pepper and garlic, stirring occasionally, for 6–8 minutes, or until softened but not browned. Add the haggis and crumble it with a wooden spoon. Cook for 2–3 minutes and then add the drained swede and spinach and cook for 2 minutes, turning once or twice, until the spinach wilts.

Beat the eggs in a bowl and season lightly with salt and pepper. Pour into the frying pan and reduce the heat. Cook gently for 5–6 minutes until the frittata is set and golden brown underneath.

Sprinkle with grated cheese and pop the pan under a preheated hot grill (broiler) for 5 minutes, or until the top is lightly browned and the tortilla is set.

Slide the cooked tortilla out of the pan onto a wooden board and let it cool a little. When it's lukewarm, cut into wedges and serve with salad.

Tip: Frittata is always best eaten warm or at room temperature, but it also makes a good packed lunch.

VARIATIONS
- Use pumpkin or butternut squash instead of swede.
- Baby spinach leaves also work well.

CHEESY HAGGIS BAKED POTATOES

Oven-baked potatoes make an easy meal. You can make the beef and haggis topping a day in advance and keep it in the fridge until you're ready to reheat it and serve.

SERVES 4
PREP 15 MINUTES
COOK 1 HOUR

4 baking potatoes, washed and scrubbed
1 tbsp olive oil, plus extra for brushing
1 onion, finely chopped
1 large carrot, diced
200g (7oz) minced (ground) beef
200g (7oz) haggis, crumbled
150ml (5fl oz/scant ¾ cup) hot beef stock
1 tbsp tomato ketchup
a dash of Worcestershire sauce
60g (2oz/¼ cup) butter
100g (3½oz/1 cup) grated Cheddar cheese
coarse sea salt and freshly ground black pepper

Preheat the oven to 200°C (180°C fan)/400°F/gas 6.

Brush the potatoes with oil and sprinkle with coarse sea salt. Place on a baking tray (sheet pan) and cook in the preheated oven for 50–60 minutes, or until the skins are crisp and the flesh inside is soft.

Meanwhile, heat the oil in a saucepan set over a medium heat. Cook the onion and carrot, stirring occasionally, for 5 minutes, or until softened. Stir in the mince and haggis and cook for 5 minutes until browned all over.

Add the stock, ketchup and Worcestershire sauce, then bring to the boil. Reduce the heat and simmer for 10–15 minutes, or until the sauce reduces and thickens. Check the seasoning, adding more ketchup or sauce if needed.

Cut a cross in the top of each cooked baked potato and push up from below with your fingers to open it up. Scoop out most of the flesh and mash in a bowl with the butter. Beat in the cheese and season to taste with salt and pepper.

Replace inside the potatoes and serve topped with the haggis and beef mixture.

> **VARIATIONS**
> - Use sweet potatoes instead of regular baking ones.
> - Add some garlic and herbs to the haggis topping.

HAGGIS PITTA POCKETS WITH TZATZIKI

Stuffed pitta breads are great for a delicious light meal or food 'on the go' when you're out and about. They also make the perfect packed lunch. You can use wraps or even flour or corn tortillas instead if you don't have any pitta breads.

SERVES 4
PREP 20 MINUTES

2 tomatoes, quartered
¼ cucumber, cut into chunks
¼ red onion, thinly sliced
8 stoned (pitted) black olives
a pinch of dried oregano
1–2 tsp olive oil
a splash of red wine vinegar
100g (3½oz) feta cheese, cubed
4 pitta breads
400g (14oz) cooked vegetarian haggis, crumbled

TZATZIKI:
200g (7oz/scant 1 cup) 0% fat Greek yoghurt
1 tbsp olive oil
½ cucumber, diced
2 garlic cloves, crushed
a handful of dill, chopped
juice of ½ lemon
sea salt and freshly ground black pepper

Make the tzatziki: mix all the ingredients together in a bowl, adding salt to taste. Chill in the refrigerator until required.

Mix together the tomatoes, cucumber, onion, olives and oregano in a bowl. Drizzle with the olive oil and vinegar and toss gently together. Stir in the feta, and season to taste.

Lightly toast the pitta breads and split them open along one long side to make a pocket. Fill them with the haggis and tomato and feta mixture, then top with tzatziki.

VARIATIONS
- Add some crisp Little Gem or Cos (romaine) lettuce.
- Substitute hummus for tzatziki.
- Fill with Haggis Meatballs (see page 84).
- Drizzle with sweet chilli sauce or Sriracha.

BAKED HAGGIS STUFFED VEGETABLES

Vegetarian haggis mixed with savoury rice makes a great filling for colourful stuffed vegetables. And because they taste best eaten warm or at room temperature, you can make them in advance – perfect for entertaining.

SERVES 4–6
PREP 15 MINUTES
COOK 1¼–1¾ HOURS

4 large beefsteak tomatoes
4 large red, yellow or green (bell) peppers
olive oil, for drizzling
crusty bread, to serve

RICE AND HAGGIS FILLING:

3 tbsp olive oil, plus extra for drizzling
2 onions, chopped
3 garlic cloves, crushed
200g (7oz) vegetarian haggis, crumbled
a good pinch of ground cinnamon
225g (8oz/1 cup) risotto rice
120ml (4fl oz/½ cup) water
1 tsp tomato paste
a handful of parsley, chopped
a pinch of sugar
sea salt and freshly ground black pepper

Preheat the oven to 200°C (180°C fan)/400°F/gas 6.

Cut the tops off the tomatoes and peppers and reserve to use as 'lids'. Scoop the seeds and pulp out of the tomatoes and set aside for the filling. Remove the white ribs and seeds from the peppers and discard.

Make the rice and haggis filling: heat the olive oil in a large frying pan (skillet) over a medium heat. Add the onion and garlic and cook, stirring occasionally, for 5 minutes. Stir in the haggis, cinnamon and rice and cook for 2 minutes. Add the water, tomato paste and reserved tomato pulp and cook over a low heat, stirring occasionally, for 5 minutes. Stir in the chopped parsley and cook for 1–2 minutes. Remove from the heat and season with sugar, salt and pepper.

Stuff the tomatoes and peppers with the rice mixture, taking care not to fill them right to the top – leave a little space as the rice will plump up while cooking. Cover with the reserved 'lids' and place in an ovenproof baking dish. Drizzle generously with olive oil.

Bake in the preheated oven for 1–1½ hours or until the tomatoes and peppers are cooked but still hold their shape and the rice is tender. Turn off the oven and leave them for 10 minutes before taking them out. Serve warm or at room temperature with crusty bread to mop up the olive oil and delicious juices.

VARIATIONS
- You can stuff aubergines (eggplants) and large courgettes (zucchini) in the same way.
- Use chopped mint or coriander (cilantro) instead of parsley.

SPICY HAGGIS TACOS

Haggis is so versatile that you can even spice it up and use it as a filling for tacos. We've used vegetarian haggis in ours but traditional haggis and beef stock work just as well.

SERVES 4
PREP 15 MINUTES
COOK 45 MINUTES

2 tbsp olive oil
1 large onion, chopped
2 garlic cloves, crushed
2 tsp hot chilli powder
400g (14oz) vegetarian haggis, crumbled
1 x 400g (14oz) can chopped tomatoes
1 tbsp tomato paste
1 x 400g (14oz) can black beans, rinsed and drained
120ml (4fl oz/½ cup) hot vegetable stock
4 taco shells
1 avocado, peeled, stoned (pitted) and smashed
½ red onion, thinly sliced
a few crisp lettuce leaves, shredded
sea salt and freshly ground black pepper

TO SERVE:
soured cream
hot tomato salsa
Mexican hot sauce
limes, for squeezing

Heat the oil in a saucepan set over a medium heat. Cook the onion and garlic, stirring occasionally, for 6–8 minutes, or until softened. Stir in the chilli powder and cook for 1 minute.

Add the haggis and cook for 5 minutes, stirring occasionally, and then add the tomatoes, tomato paste, beans and stock. Cover the pan and simmer for 15 minutes. Remove the lid and cook, uncovered, for another 15 minutes, or until the sauce has reduced and thickened. Season to taste with salt and pepper.

Meanwhile, crisp up the taco shells by placing them on a baking tray (sheet pan) and warming in a preheated oven at 180°C (160°C fan)/350°F/gas 4 for 2–3 minutes.

Divide the haggis mixture among the taco shells and top with the smashed avocado, red onion and shredded lettuce.

Serve hot with bowls of soured cream and salsa with some hot sauce for drizzling and fresh limes for squeezing.

VARIATIONS
- Instead of using taco shells, wrap the haggis filling, avocado, red onion and lettuce in corn or flour tortillas.
- Add some diced red (bell) pepper to the spicy haggis mixture.
- Swap the black beans for red kidney beans.

VEGGIE HAGGIS BALLS WITH RICE

All the family, kids included, will love these veggie meatballs. They're so quick and easy to make. You can also use them as a filling for wraps and pitta bread or pop any leftover cold ones into a lunchbox for a packed lunch.

SERVES 4
PREP 10 MINUTES
COOK 30 MINUTES

450g (1lb) cooked vegetarian haggis, crumbled
½ onion, grated
2 garlic cloves, crushed
30g (1oz/¼ cup) grated Parmesan cheese
a handful of parsley, finely chopped
1 large free-range egg, beaten
vegetable oil, for brushing
sea salt and freshly ground black pepper
boiled rice, to serve

EASY-PEASY TOMATO SAUCE:
2 tbsp olive oil
450g (1lb) cherry or baby plum tomatoes
a good pinch of sugar
a few sprigs of basil, torn

Preheat the oven to 190°C (170°C fan)/375°F/gas 5.

Crumble the haggis into a bowl and stir in the onion, garlic, Parmesan and parsley. Add the beaten egg and seasoning and mix until well combined.

Divide the mixture into 12 equal-sized portions and, using your hands, roll each one into a smooth ball.

Brush a baking tray (sheet pan) with oil and arrange the meatballs on it, leaving some space around each one. Bake in the preheated oven for 30 minutes, turning them once or twice, until golden brown and crisp and cooked right through.

Meanwhile, make the tomato sauce: heat the olive oil in a large frying pan (skillet) set over a medium heat. Add the tomatoes and cook, turning and stirring them occasionally, for 5 minutes, or until they start to soften. Press down gently on them with a spatula to squash them and release their juice. Add the sugar and season with salt and pepper.

Reduce the heat and simmer gently for 5 minutes or until the sauce reduces and thickens. Stir in the basil.

Serve the meatballs in four bowls on a bed of rice and spoon the tomato sauce over the top.

> **VARIATIONS**
> • Serve with pasta instead of rice.
> • Use Cheddar instead of Parmesan.
> • Drizzle with some pesto.

THE FULL SCOTTISH

You've heard of the 'full English' breakfast and now you can try our Scottish version, which is equally delicious and nutritious. We've added some spinach and grated cheese for extra colour and flavour, and to make it easy with less washing up, we've used just one pan. It's a win win!

SERVES 4
PREP 10 MINUTES
COOK 15 MINUTES

olive oil, for brushing
400g (14oz) open field or chestnut mushrooms
8 slices of lean smoked back bacon
4 slices of haggis (see note)
8 cherry or baby plum tomatoes, halved
100g (3½oz) baby spinach leaves
4 medium free-range eggs
100g (3½oz/1 cup) grated Cheddar cheese (optional)
sea salt and freshly ground black pepper
buttered toast, to serve
tomato ketchup, brown sauce and mustard, to serve

Note: You can buy prepared haggis slices from some butchers or in packs from many supermarkets.

Preheat the oven to 200°C (180°C fan)/400°F/gas 6.

Lightly brush a large non-stick roasting pan with oil. Add the mushrooms, open-side down, bacon, haggis and tomatoes and cook for 10 minutes in the preheated oven.

Meanwhile, put the spinach in a colander and pour boiling water over so the leaves wilt and turn bright green. Pat dry with kitchen paper (paper towels) to remove any excess water.

Turn over the mushrooms, bacon and haggis and arrange little heaps of spinach around the tomatoes and mushrooms. Make four spaces between them and crack an egg into each one. Season with salt and pepper and sprinkle the cheese (if using) over the vegetables.

Bake in the oven for 5 minutes, or until the egg whites are set but the yolks are still runny, and the cheese has melted.

Serve immediately with buttered toast and everyone can help themselves to ketchup, brown sauce and mustard.

Tip: This also makes a great brunch or light lunch and the recipe can easily be halved for two people.

VARIATIONS
- Instead of bacon, use leftover diced cooked potatoes and cubed tofu for a veggie version.
- Add some chipolata (link) sausages (pork, turkey or Quorn).
- Swap some diced chorizo or pancetta cubes for the bacon.
- Add some sliced black pudding.

MAIN MEALS

HAGGIS WELLINGTON

A filling and warming dish that's perfect for a cold winter's day. Enjoy it with family and friends on Burns Night or as a substitute for your usual Sunday roast. It looks impressive but is actually very easy to make.

SERVES 4
PREP 20 MINUTES
COOK 50–55 MINUTES

1 tbsp olive oil
30g (1oz/2 tbsp) butter
300g (10oz) white or chestnut mushrooms, diced
a pinch of dried mixed herbs
1 x 375g (13oz) pack of ready-rolled puff pastry
plain (all-purpose) flour, for dusting
500g (1lb 2oz) haggis
1 medium free-range egg, beaten
sea salt and freshly ground black pepper

TO SERVE:
green vegetables and carrots
Gravy (see pages 20–22) or Whisky Sauce (see page 23)

VARIATIONS
- Use a vegetarian haggis instead.
- Add a layer of mashed or thinly sliced cooked swede (rutabaga) on top of the mushrooms.

Preheat the oven to 200°C (180°C fan)/400°F/gas 6. Line a baking tray (sheet pan) with baking parchment.

Heat the oil and butter in a large frying pan (skillet) set over a low to medium heat and cook the mushrooms, turning occasionally, for 6–8 minutes, or until tender and golden brown. Season lightly with salt and pepper and stir in the herbs.

Roll out the pastry on a lightly floured surface to a large rectangle – it should be about 3mm (⅛ inch) thick. Spoon the mushroom mixture lengthways down the centre of the pastry and place the haggis on top.

Brush the border of the pastry rectangle with beaten egg and fold the pastry over the top, pressing down to seal the edges together. Crimp with a fork and then tuck in the ends. Place on the lined baking tray and lightly brush the pastry all over with beaten egg.

Bake in the preheated oven for 40–45 minutes, or until the pastry is puffed up, golden brown and crisp. Serve, cut into slices, with green vegetables and carrots, and a jug of gravy or whisky sauce.

Note: If using a bought haggis, remove the casing before placing it on top of the mushrooms.

Tip: You can make the haggis into a sausage shape to fit the pastry by wrapping it between three to four layers of cling film (plastic wrap) and rolling it to the desired length. Chill in the refrigerator for 20–30 minutes and unwrap just before use.

HAGGIS SAUSAGES WITH RED CABBAGE

Haggis and red cabbage are a marriage made in culinary heaven. The spicy sweetness of the red cabbage perfectly complements the savoury sausages.

SERVES 4
PREP 10 MINUTES
COOK 1¼ HOURS

8 vegetarian Haggis Sausages (see page 16)
mashed or baked potatoes, to serve

RED CABBAGE:
25g (1oz/2 tbsp) butter
1 red onion, diced
1 small red cabbage, quartered, cored and leaves shredded
2 large cooking apples, e.g. Bramleys, peeled, cored and chopped
grated zest and juice of 2 oranges
3 tbsp red wine vinegar
60g (2oz/¼ cup) soft brown sugar
a good pinch of ground cinnamon or nutmeg
sea salt and freshly ground black pepper

Make the red cabbage: melt the butter in a flameproof casserole set over a low to medium heat. Cook the onion, stirring occasionally, for 5 minutes, or until softened.

Stir in the red cabbage and chopped apple and pour in sufficient boiling water to cover the base of the casserole. Stir in the orange zest and juice, vinegar, sugar and ground spice, and season with salt and pepper.

Cover with a lid and increase the heat to high. When the water boils, reduce the heat to low and simmer gently for 1 hour, or until the cabbage is tender and the liquid has evaporated. Alternatively, you can cook it in a low oven at 150°C (130°C fan)/300°F/gas 2.

When the red cabbage is nearly ready, cook the haggis sausages in the oven, or on the hob in a frying pan (skillet) or griddle pan or under a preheated hot grill (broiler) according to the instructions on the packet, until cooked and browned.

Serve the sausages with the red cabbage and some mashed or baked potatoes.

Tip: Some sharp hot mustard goes well with the sausages.

VARIATIONS
- Stir some cranberries into the red cabbage as it cooks.
- Add a little red wine with the boiling water.
- Serve the sausages with cooked brown lentils.

HAGGIS CHICKEN KIEV

Our haggis chicken Kievs are garlicky, buttery and oozing with flavour. They are easy to make and a great source of protein. Serve them with a crunchy salad or some baked potatoes and green vegetables.

SERVES 4
PREP 20 MINUTES
FREEZE 15 MINUTES
COOK 20-25 MINUTES

4 x 150g (5oz) skinned and boned chicken breasts
175g (6oz) cooked haggis
2 tbsp plain (all-purpose) flour
1 large free-range egg, beaten
100g (3½oz/1 cup) panko breadcrumbs
spray olive oil
sea salt and freshly ground black pepper

GARLIC BUTTER:
60g (2oz/¼ cup) butter, softened
4 garlic cloves, crushed
4 tbsp chopped parsley

Make the garlic butter: mix the butter, garlic and parsley in a bowl. Shape into a cylinder and wrap tightly in cling film (plastic wrap). Freeze for 15 minutes, or until frozen.

Preheat the oven to 200°C (180°C fan)/400°F/gas 6.

With a sharp knife, cut a small horizontal opening in the side of each chicken breast and slide in your fingers to make a deep pocket. Divide the haggis into four equal-sized portions and stuff a portion into each chicken breast.

Cut the frozen garlic butter into four slices and place one slice in each chicken pocket on top of the haggis, pushing everything in well so that you can press the top and bottom edges of the chicken together to close and seal the slit. Season with salt and pepper.

Lightly dust the chicken breasts with flour and then dip into the beaten egg before coating with the breadcrumbs.

Place on a baking tray (sheet pan) and lightly spray them with oil. Cook in the preheated oven for 20–25 minutes, turning them after 10 minutes, until crisp, golden brown and cooked right through. Serve immediately.

Tip: Don't cut a long slit along the side of the chicken as the filling is more likely to spill out.

VARIATIONS
- Add some grated Parmesan cheese to the breadcrumbs.
- Serve with ketchup, hot sauce or some cranberry sauce.

HAGGIS BURRITO NIGHT DINNER

Haggis burritos are fun to assemble and perfect for weeknight dinners and TV suppers. They are very flexible and a great way to use up leftovers (cooked haggis, rice, canned beans, salad vegetables). Adding haggis to burritos may sound unusual, but its spicy flavour complements the Mexican ingredients and is enhanced by the pico de gallo.

SERVES 4
PREP 15 MINUTES
COOK 15 MINUTES

150g (5oz/⅔ cup) basmati rice
8 soft tortilla wraps
a few Little Gem or Cos (romaine) lettuce leaves, shredded
200g (7oz) vegetarian haggis
1 x 400g (14oz) can black beans, rinsed and drained
1 ripe avocado, peeled, stoned (pitted) and diced
juice of ½ lime
8 tbsp grated Cheddar cheese
120g (4oz/½ cup) soured cream
a small handful of coriander (cilantro), chopped
Tabasco or hot sauce, for drizzling
lime quarters, for squeezing

PICO DE GALLO:
4 large ripe tomatoes, diced
1 red onion, diced
1–2 hot chillies, e.g. jalapenos, diced (fresh or bottled)
1 bunch of coriander (cilantro), finely chopped
juice of 1 lime
½ tsp sea salt flakes

Make the pico de gallo: mix everything together in a bowl and leave for at least 15 minutes for the flavours to mingle. Store in a sealed container in the fridge. It keeps well for 24 hours.

Cook the rice as per the instructions on the packet.

Warm the tortilla wraps in the microwave or on a griddle pan set over a low heat.

To assemble the wraps: place a line of lettuce down the centre of each wrap and spoon the warm cooked rice over the top. Add the haggis and black beans.

Pour the lime juice over the avocado and stir gently. Add to the tortillas with some pico de gallo. Sprinkle with grated cheese and top with a spoonful of soured cream and a sprinkle of coriander.

Roll up the tortillas or fold in the ends to enclose the filling and then roll. Serve drizzled with Tabasco or hot sauce with some lime quarters for squeezing.

Tip: Alternatively, you can divide the filling ingredients among serving bowls and let everyone roll their own tortillas.

VARIATIONS
- Use Greek or non-dairy yoghurt instead of soured cream.
- Buy a jar or carton of ready-made salsa if you don't have time to make pico de gallo.
- Use red kidney beans or refried beans instead of black ones.
- Substitute quinoa or couscous for the rice.

HAGGIS HOTPOT

Topped with a layer of crispy golden potatoes, a hotpot makes a great supper on a cold winter's day. We've used chicken instead of the traditional lamb and added haggis for extra flavour. It's so good that you could serve it for your special Burns Night dinner.

SERVES 4
PREP 20 MINUTES
COOK 1¾–2 HOURS

- 2–3 tbsp olive oil
- 250g (9oz) skinned chicken breasts, cubed
- 200g (7oz) haggis, diced
- 1 large onion, thinly sliced
- 2 leeks, cleaned, trimmed and thinly sliced
- 2 carrots, sliced
- 2 garlic cloves, crushed
- 2 tbsp plain (all-purpose) flour
- 120ml (4fl oz/½ cup) medium or dry white wine
- 420ml (14fl oz/1¾ cups) hot chicken stock
- a few drops of white wine vinegar or cider vinegar
- a handful of flat-leaf parsley, chopped
- 900g (2lb) potatoes, peeled and thinly sliced into rounds
- 30g (1oz/2 tbsp) butter, melted
- sea salt and freshly ground black pepper

Heat the oil in a deep, large frying pan (skillet) or sauté pan (or flameproof casserole dish) set over a medium heat. Add the chicken and cook, turning occasionally, for 5 minutes, or until it is golden brown all over. Remove the chicken and set aside.

Add the haggis to the hot pan and cook, stirring occasionally, for 5 minutes. Remove from the pan and set aside with the chicken.

Add the onion, leeks and carrots to the pan and reduce the heat to low. Cook, stirring occasionally, for 10 minutes, or until softened. Add the garlic and cook for 2 minutes, then stir in the flour.

Add the wine and increase the heat to medium to high. Let it bubble away until most of it has evaporated and then pour in the stock and a dash of vinegar.

Preheat the oven to 180°C (160°C fan)/350°F/gas 4.

Return the chicken and haggis to the pan and cook, stirring occasionally, over a medium heat until the sauce starts to reduce and thicken a little. Stir in the parsley and season with salt and pepper. Transfer to an ovenproof casserole dish.

Arrange the potato slices in overlapping circles over the top of the chicken and haggis mixture. Cover with kitchen foil or a lid and cook in the preheated oven for 1–1¼ hours until the potatoes are tender. Remove the foil or lid and brush the potatoes with melted butter.

Increase the oven temperature to 200°C (180°C fan)/400°F/gas 6 and return to the oven for 10–15 minutes, or until the potatoes are crisp and appetizingly golden brown.

HAGGIS CHILLI SALSA POT

The addition of haggis to a pan of chilli enhances the flavour and you can give it a real kick by stirring in some freshly made Mexican tomato salsa.

SERVES 4
PREP 15 MINUTES
COOK 35–40 MINUTES

1 tbsp olive oil
1 large onion, chopped
1 red (bell) pepper, deseeded and diced
3 garlic cloves, crushed
300g (10oz) minced (ground) beef
2 tsp chilli powder
1 tsp ground cumin
1 tsp sweet paprika
1 x 400g (14oz) can chopped tomatoes
240ml (8fl oz/1 cup) hot beef stock
1 x 400g (14oz) can kidney beans
200g (7oz) haggis, crumbled
boiled rice, soured cream and grated Cheddar cheese, to serve

SPICY TOMATO SALSA:
4 ripe tomatoes, diced
¼ red onion, diced
1–2 hot chillies, e.g. jalapenos, diced (fresh or bottled)
a large handful of coriander (cilantro), chopped
juice of 1 lime
sea salt and black pepper

Make the spicy tomato salsa: mix everything together in a bowl. Check the seasoning, adding more lime juice or salt, if wished. Cover and set aside.

Heat the oil in a saucepan set over a low to medium heat. Cook the onion, red pepper and garlic, stirring occasionally, for 8–10 minutes until tender.

Stir in the minced beef and ground spices and cook, stirring occasionally, for 5 minutes until the beef is browned all over. Add the tomatoes and stock and bring to the boil.

Drain and rinse the kidney beans. Reduce the heat to low and add the haggis and beans. Simmer gently for 20–25 minutes or until the vegetables are tender and the liquid has reduced and thickened. Stir in the tomato salsa and season to taste with salt and pepper.

Serve hot with some boiled rice in shallow bowls, sprinkled with grated cheese and topped with soured cream.

VARIATIONS
- Use bottled or freshly made supermarket salsa.
- Serve with chunky guacamole or diced avocado.
- Instead of rice, serve with warmed flatbreads, wraps or tortillas.
- Add some sweetcorn kernels.

HAGGIS TOAD IN THE HOLE

The secret to success is to make sure the oil or fat is smoking hot when you pour in the batter. This will crisp up the base of the Yorkshire pudding – you don't want it to be soggy.

SERVES 4
PREP 10 MINUTES
STAND 30 MINUTES
COOK 35–45 MINUTES

175g (6oz/1¾ cups) plain (all-purpose) flour
¼ tsp salt
4 large free-range eggs, beaten
420ml (14fl oz/1¾ cups) milk
1–2 tbsp vegetable oil or meat dripping
8 Haggis Sausages (shop bought or see page 16)
Onion Gravy, to serve (see page 21)
buttered cabbage or Brussels sprouts, to serve

Make the batter: sift the flour and salt into a bowl and make a well in the centre. Add the eggs with a little milk. Beat together and then gradually beat in the rest of the milk until you have a smooth batter without any lumps and the consistency of thin cream. Pour into a jug and leave to stand for 30 minutes.

Preheat the oven to 220°C (200°C fan)/425°F/gas 7.

Put 1 tablespoon oil or dripping in a large roasting pan – about 30 x 25cm (12 x 10 inches) – and place in the hot oven for 5–10 minutes, or until it is sizzling and smoking.

Add the sausages and cook in the oven for 5–6 minutes until browned underneath. Turn them over and cook on the other side for 5–6 minutes until browned. If there's not much fat in the pan, add another tablespoon of oil or dripping.

Quickly pour in the batter and return the pan to the oven immediately. Bake for 25–30 minutes, or until the batter is well-risen, golden brown and crisp on top. Do *not* open the oven door while it is cooking or it may collapse.

Cut the Yorkshire into four pieces (each with two sausages) and serve with onion gravy and some buttered cabbage or Brussels sprouts.

Tip: You can beat the batter by hand, use a hand-held electric whisk or make it in a blender or food processor.

VARIATIONS
- Add some chopped or dried herbs to the batter.
- Serve with mustard or horseradish.

HAGGIS AND GARLICKY SPRING ONION MASH

Sausage and mash is the ultimate comfort food on a cold day – it's soothing, sustaining and simple to make. We've used delicious vegetarian haggis sausages, but you can swap them for traditional meaty ones.

SERVES 4
PREP 10 MINUTES
COOK 20–25 MINUTES

900g (2lb) potatoes, e.g. Maris Piper or King Edward, peeled and cut into large chunks
75ml (3fl oz/generous ¼ cup) milk
15g (½oz/1 tbsp) butter
4 spring onions (scallions), finely sliced
2–3 garlic cloves, crushed
8 vegetarian Haggis Sausages (see page 16)
sea salt and freshly ground black pepper
green beans, broccoli, cabbage or Brussels sprouts, to serve

CARAMELIZED ONION GRAVY:

3 tbsp olive oil
2 large onions, thinly sliced
2 tbsp plain (all-purpose) flour
300ml (½ pint/1¼ cups) hot vegetable stock
1–2 tbsp syrupy balsamic vinegar

Half-fill a large pan with salted water and bring to the boil. Add the potatoes and boil for 12–15 minutes, until tender. Drain well in a colander and then return to the hot pan with the milk and butter.

Off the heat, mash the potatoes and beat with a wooden spoon or an electric whisk until smooth, creamy and lump-free. Stir in the spring onions and garlic and season to taste with salt and pepper. Keep warm.

Make the gravy: heat the oil in a frying pan set over a low heat. Add the onions and cook for 15 minutes, stirring occasionally, until meltingly tender and starting to caramelize. Stir in the flour and cook for 1 minute. Gradually stir in the stock and vinegar and increase the heat to high. Bring to the boil, stirring, then reduce the heat and simmer gently for 4–5 minutes, or until thickened and smooth. Season to taste with salt and pepper.

Meanwhile, cook the sausages in a frying pan (skillet) set over a medium heat, turning once or twice, until golden brown all over and cooked through.

Serve the sausages with the mashed potato and onion gravy with some green vegetables.

VARIATIONS
- Use red onions instead of white in the gravy.
- Instead of balsamic vinegar use red or white wine vinegar and sweeten with redcurrant jelly or cranberry sauce.
- Cook the sausages in an air fryer in a single layer, leaving a little space between them. Cook for 10–12 minutes, turning them two to three times.

VEGAN HAGGIS CURRY

If you've never considered adding haggis to a curry, now is the time to try. You can buy a vegetarian haggis that is suitable for vegans in many supermarkets and delis or online. Check the listed ingredients on the label. We've added non-dairy yoghurt for a creamy sauce.

SERVES 4
PREP 10 MINUTES
COOK 30–35 MINUTES

3 tbsp vegetable oil
1 large onion, chopped
1 large leek, cleaned, trimmed and thinly sliced
3 garlic cloves, crushed
2.5cm (1 inch) piece of fresh root ginger, peeled and grated
2 red or green chillies, diced
500g (1lb 2oz) vegan haggis (see above)
1 x 400g (14oz) can chopped tomatoes
1 x 400g (14oz) can chickpeas (garbanzos), rinsed and drained
2 tsp ground cumin
1 tsp ground coriander
1 tsp ground turmeric
1 tsp garam masala
120g (4oz/½ cup) non-dairy yoghurt
a handful of mint, finely chopped
a handful of coriander (cilantro), finely chopped
sea salt and freshly ground black pepper
boiled rice, to serve

Heat the oil in a large frying pan (skillet) set over a medium heat. Add the onion and leek and cook, stirring occasionally, for 6–8 minutes until tender. Stir in the garlic, ginger and chillies and cook for 2–3 minutes.

Crumble in the haggis and cook, stirring often to prevent it sticking to the pan, for 6–8 minutes. Add the canned tomatoes and chickpeas and cook for 10 minutes.

Add the ground spices and yoghurt and cook for 5 minutes. Season to taste with salt and pepper.

Stir in the mint and coriander and serve hot with boiled rice.

VARIATIONS
- For a creamier curry, add more yoghurt.
- If you don't have fresh chillies, use crushed red chillies or chilli paste.
- Add some frozen peas.
- Vary the spices: try adding ground cinnamon, cloves or curry powder.

HAGGIS, SWEDE AND SPINACH FILO PIE

This delicious savoury pie is encased in a crisp filo (phyllo) pastry crust. We've used vegetarian haggis and vegans can substitute olive oil for melted butter.

SERVES 4–6
PREP 20 MINUTES
COOK 45–50 MINUTES

2 tbsp olive oil, plus extra for brushing
450g (1lb) swede (rutabaga), peeled and diced
1 large onion, diced
1 garlic clove, crushed
200g (7oz) spinach leaves, washed, trimmed and shredded
8 sheets of ready-rolled filo (phyllo) pastry
60g (2oz/¼ cup) unsalted butter, melted
400g (14oz) vegetarian haggis
sea salt and freshly ground black pepper

Preheat the oven to 190°C (170°C fan)/375°F/gas 5. Lightly brush a 30 x 20cm (12 x 8 inches) baking tray (sheet pan) with oil.

Cook the swede in a pan of boiling water set over a high heat for 12–15 minutes, or until tender but not mushy.

Meanwhile, heat the olive oil in a large saucepan set over a low to medium heat and cook the onion and garlic, stirring occasionally, for 8–10 minutes, or until softened. Add the spinach leaves and stir well. Cover the pan and cook for 2–3 minutes, or until the leaves wilt. Season to taste with salt and pepper.

Unfold the filo pastry and cover with a damp clean cloth to prevent it drying out. Cover the bottom of the oiled baking pan with one sheet of pastry and brush lightly with melted butter. Add another three sheets, brushing with butter each time.

Spoon the swede and onion and spinach mixture over the pastry. Crumble the haggis over the top in a single layer and then cover with another sheet of pastry. Brush with melted butter and add the remaining sheets, brushing with butter each time.

Lightly score the top in a diamond pattern with a sharp knife and brush with any remaining butter or olive oil.

Bake in the preheated oven for 30–35 minutes, or until the pastry is crisp and golden brown. Remove and cool slightly before cutting into squares.

> **VARIATIONS**
> - Add some chopped herbs, e.g. parsley, sage or even dill.
> - Serve hot or at room temperature with vegetables or a crisp salad.

HAGGIS CHEESEBURGERS

Nothing beats a tasty, juicy cheeseburger and you can make them even more interesting and delicious by adding haggis to the beef mixture.

SERVES 4
PREP 15 MINUTES
CHILL 30 MINUTES
COOK 11–14 MINUTES

250g (9oz) good-quality minced (ground) beef
250g (9oz) haggis, crumbled
vegetable oil, for oiling
4 thick slices of Cheddar cheese
4 burger buns, split and toasted
4 tsp mayonnaise
crisp Cos (romaine) or iceberg lettuce, shredded
1 beefsteak tomato, sliced
½ red onion, thinly sliced
2 dill pickles, sliced
sea salt and freshly ground black pepper
mustard, tomato ketchup and relish, to serve

Put the minced beef and haggis in a bowl and mix well.

Divide the mixture into four equal-sized portions and mould each one into a round burger patty with your hands. Cover and chill in the fridge for at least 30 minutes to firm them up.

When you're ready to cook, set a lightly oiled griddle pan or frying pan (skillet) over a medium to high heat or fire up the barbecue and lightly oil the grill.

Lightly sprinkle the burgers with a little salt and pepper and place them in the hot pan or on the grill. Reduce the heat to medium and cook for 5–6 minutes, until well seared and starting to char underneath. Flip the burgers over and place a slice of cheese on top of each one. Cook for 6–8 minutes, until the cheese melts and the burgers are done to your liking.

Spread the mayonnaise over the toasted base of each bun and add the lettuce, tomato and red onion. Place a cheeseburger on top of each and add some sliced dill pickles. Cover with the top halves of the buns and serve immediately with mustard or tomato ketchup.

Tip: If the beef and haggis are a bit crumbly, bind them together with a little beaten egg.

VARIATIONS
- Add some cooked crispy bacon slices.
- Add some fried onions – try caramelized red onions.
- Serve with French fries or thick-cut chips.
- Swap Swiss cheese for the Cheddar.

HAGGIS SHEPHERD'S PIE

A tasty and warming dish for all the family – your children will love this haggis pie topped with tatties and neeps (mashed potatoes and swede). You can make one large pie or smaller individual ones. Vegetarian haggis works equally well – make with vegetable stock.

SERVES 4-6
PREP 20 MINUTES
COOK 1¼ HOURS

2 tbsp olive oil
1 large onion, finely chopped
2 celery sticks, chopped
2 large carrots, diced
1 garlic clove, crushed
500g (1lb 2oz) haggis, crumbled
1 tbsp tomato paste
2 tbsp tomato ketchup
2 tbsp Worcestershire sauce
300ml (½ pint/1¼ cups) hot beef stock
1 heaped tbsp cornflour (cornstarch)
450g (1lb) potatoes, peeled and cut into large chunks
300g (10oz) swede (rutabaga), peeled and cut into chunks
60g (2oz/¼ cup) butter, plus extra for topping
120ml (4fl oz/½ cup) milk
60g (2oz/½ cup) grated Cheddar cheese
sea salt and freshly ground black pepper

Heat the olive oil in a saucepan set over a medium heat and cook the onion, celery, carrots and garlic for 8–10 minutes, or until softened.

Stir in the haggis, tomato paste, ketchup, Worcestershire sauce and stock and bring to the boil. Reduce the heat to low and simmer gently for 30 minutes. Blend the cornflour with a little water to make a smooth paste and stir into the haggis mixture to thicken it. Transfer to a baking dish and level the top.

While the haggis is cooking, boil the potatoes and swede in separate pans of salted water until cooked and tender. Drain well and return to their respective pans.

Preheat the oven to 200°C (180°C fan)/400°F/gas 6.

Mash the potatoes and swede separately with the butter and milk until smooth and lump-free. Combine the two mixtures in a bowl and season to taste with salt and pepper.

Spoon the mash over the haggis mixture and fluff it up with a fork. Sprinkle with grated Cheddar and dot the top with small pieces of butter.

Place the baking dish on a baking tray (sheet pan) or inside a roasting pan and bake in the preheated oven for 25–30 minutes, or until crisp and golden brown.

> **VARIATIONS**
> • Add some frozen peas to the haggis filling.
> • Add a splash of red wine with the beef stock.
> • Substitute potatoes for the swede.

HAGGIS MEATBALLS AND SPAGHETTI

Nearly everyone, especially children, loves spaghetti and meatballs, but have you ever considered making them with haggis?

SERVES 1
PREP 20 MINUTES
COOK 35–40 MINUTES

250g (9oz) minced (ground) beef (not too lean)
250g (9oz) haggis, crumbled
25g (1oz/½ cup) fresh white breadcrumbs
50g (2oz/½ cup) grated Parmesan, plus extra for sprinkling
2 garlic cloves, crushed
1 medium free-range egg, beaten
1 small onion, grated
a handful of parsley, chopped
4 tbsp olive oil, plus extra for shallow-frying
400g (14oz) spaghetti
sea salt and freshly ground black pepper

MARINARA SAUCE:
2 tbsp olive oil
1 onion, diced
3 garlic cloves, crushed
2 x 400g (14oz) cans chopped tomatoes
a good pinch of dried oregano
a good pinch of sugar

Make the meatballs: put the beef and haggis in a bowl with the breadcrumbs, Parmesan, garlic, egg, onion, parsley, olive oil, salt and pepper. Mix it up with your hands, scrunching it together.

Take a small amount of the mixture and, with your hands, roll it into a ball, a little larger than a walnut and smaller than a golf ball. Repeat with the remaining mixture. You should end up with about 16 meatballs.

Heat 3–4 tablespoons olive oil in a large frying pan (skillet) set over a medium heat and cook half of the meatballs for 3 minutes until they are well browned underneath. Turn them over and brown the other side. Don't worry if they're a bit crispy – it adds to the texture and flavour. Remove with a slotted spoon and set aside while you cook the remaining meatballs.

Meanwhile, make the tomato sauce: heat the oil in a frying pan set over a low to medium heat and cook the onion and garlic for 8–10 minutes, until softened. Add the meatballs, tomatoes, oregano and sugar and simmer gently for 15–20 minutes, or until the meatballs are cooked and the sauce thickens and reduces. Season with salt and pepper to taste.

Cook the spaghetti in a large pan of salted water according to the instructions on the packet. Drain in a colander, then add to the sauce and toss gently until everything is well coated.

Divide among four shallow bowls and serve immediately, sprinkled with grated Parmesan.

VARIATIONS
- Use linguine instead of spaghetti.
- Add some torn basil leaves and crushed red chillies to the sauce.
- Sprinkle with chopped parsley just before serving.

HAGGIS LASAGNE

Everyone loves lasagne but did you know that you can make it with haggis? Adding haggis with the minced beef makes the ragu even richer and tastier. Try it and see for yourself.

SERVES 6
PREP 25 MINUTES
COOK 3 HOURS

30g (1oz/2 tbsp) butter, for greasing and dicing
300g (10oz) dried precooked lasagne sheets (about 15 sheets)
100g (3½oz/1 cup) grated Parmesan
green salad, to serve

RAGU SAUCE:
3 tbsp olive oil
1 large onion, finely chopped
3 garlic cloves, crushed
3 celery sticks, chopped
3 carrots, chopped
400g (14oz) minced (ground) beef
250g (9oz) haggis
240ml (8fl oz/1 cup) milk
a pinch of freshly grated nutmeg
240ml (8fl oz/1 cup) dry white wine
2 x 400g (14oz) cans chopped tomatoes
sea salt and black pepper

WHITE SAUCE:
100g (3½oz/½ cup) butter
100g (3½oz/1 cup) plain (all-purpose) flour
900ml (1½ pints/3¾ cups) milk
a pinch of freshly grated nutmeg

Make the ragu sauce: heat the oil in a large pan set over a medium heat and cook the onion, stirring occasionally, until softened. Stir in the garlic, celery and carrots, and cook for 5 minutes.

Add the beef and cook for 5 minutes, stirring occasionally, until browned. Stir in the haggis and then add the milk and cook gently until there's no liquid left in the pan. Add the nutmeg and season. Add the wine and, when it evaporates, stir in the tomatoes.

Reduce the heat to low and cook for 2 hours, or until the sauce has thickened and is richly coloured. Check occasionally to make sure it's not too dry. Add some beef stock or water if necessary.

Meanwhile, make the white sauce: melt the butter in a pan set over a low heat. Stir in the flour with a wooden spoon until you have a soft paste. Cook for 2 minutes without browning, then add the milk, a little at a time, stirring until smooth. Cook for 5 minutes, still stirring, until the sauce thickens and coats the back of the spoon. Season with nutmeg and salt and pepper.

Preheat the oven to 200°C (180°C fan)/400°F/gas 6.

Assemble the lasagne: generously butter a large deep ovenproof dish and line the bottom with one-third of the lasagne sheets, laying them edge to edge. Cover with a thin layer of white sauce, sprinkle with a little Parmesan and then spoon over half of the ragu. Repeat with another layer of lasagne sheets, a thin layer of béchamel, a sprinkle of Parmesan, and the remaining ragu. Cover with the remaining pasta sheets and pour over the rest of the white sauce over the top to cover them. Sprinkle with the remaining Parmesan and dot with butter.

Bake in the preheated oven for 40 minutes, or until bubbling and golden brown on top. Set aside to stand for 10 minutes. Serve the lasagne, cut into slices or squares, with a crisp salad.

ROAST CHICKEN WITH HAGGIS STUFFING

What could be nicer on a cold day than succulent, juicy roast chicken filled with an aromatic haggis stuffing and served with crispy roast potatoes and bashed neeps (mashed buttery swede)? If you're cooking for a crowd, get a bigger chicken and cook more vegetables – cabbage, broccoli and some carrots.

SERVES 4
PREP 20 MINUTES
COOK 1½ HOURS

1 x 1.5kg (3lb 5oz) free-range chicken, at room temperature
a few sprigs of thyme and rosemary
60g (2oz/¼ cup) softened butter
olive oil, for drizzling
500g (1lb 2oz) potatoes, peeled and cut into large chunks
1 large swede (rutabaga), peeled and cut into cubes
3–4 tbsp milk or cream
sea salt and freshly ground black pepper
Gravy (see pages 20–22), to serve

HAGGIS STUFFING:

2 tbsp olive oil
1 large onion, finely chopped
leaves from a sprig of sage, chopped
leaves stripped from 2 sprigs of thyme
1 garlic clove, crushed
400g (14oz) haggis

Make the haggis stuffing: heat the olive oil in a frying pan (skillet) set over a low to medium heat. Add the onion, herbs and garlic and cook, stirring occasionally, for 8–10 minutes, or until the onion is translucent and softened. Crumble in the haggis and stir well.

Preheat the oven to 200°C (180°C fan)/400°F/gas 6.

Fill the body cavity of the chicken with the haggis stuffing and the herb sprigs. Rub half of the softened butter over the skin and place in a roasting pan. Drizzle generously with olive oil and season with salt and pepper.

Roast in the preheated oven for 1¼ hours, or until the skin is golden brown and crisp and the juices run clear when you insert a thin skewer into the thigh. Remove the roast chicken from the oven and transfer to a carving dish. Cover with kitchen foil and leave to rest for at least 15 minutes.

Meanwhile, boil the potatoes in a pan of salted water for about 5 minutes. Drain in a colander and shake them gently to soften the edges. Sprinkle lightly with salt and place them around the chicken. Turn them in the hot fat and roast, turning them occasionally, for 45–60 minutes, or until crisp and golden brown. Remove from the pan and keep warm.

Cook the swede in a pan of boiling salted water for 15 minutes or until tender. Alternatively, you can steam it for 15 minutes. Drain in a colander for 3–4 minutes and then return to the pan and mash with the remaining butter and the milk or cream. Season well with plenty of black pepper.

Carve the chicken and serve with the haggis stuffing, roast potatoes and swede with some gravy on the side.

CHEESY HAGGIS YORKSHIRES

Serve these loaded individual Yorkshires for supper with seasonal vegetables and gravy. If you're in a hurry, you can use bought ready-made frozen Yorkshire puddings and microwave the haggis.

SERVES 4
PREP 15 MINUTES
STAND 30 MINUTES
COOK 25–30 MINUTES
   + COOKING THE HAGGIS

125g (4½oz/1¼ cups) plain (all-purpose) flour
¼ tsp salt
3 large free-range eggs, beaten
240ml (8fl oz/1 cup) milk
60g (2oz/½ cup) grated Cheddar cheese
400g (14oz) vegetarian haggis
4 tsp vegetable oil
4 tbsp red onion chutney
Onion Gravy, to serve (see page 21)

Note: You will need a non-stick deep 4-cup 23 x 23cm (9 x 9 inch) Yorkshire pudding pan.

Make a batter: sift the flour and salt into a bowl. Beat in the eggs and a little milk. Gradually whisk in the remaining milk until you have a smooth batter. Transfer to a jug and leave to stand for 30 minutes. Gently stir in the grated cheese.

Meanwhile, preheat the oven to 220°C (200°C fan)/425°F/gas 7.

Cook the haggis according to the instructions on the packet.

Put 1 teaspoon vegetable oil in each of the four cups in the Yorkshire pudding pan and place in the preheated oven for 5–10 minutes, until the oil is smoking and sizzling hot.

Quickly pour the batter into the cups and place in the oven immediately. Bake for 20–25 minutes, or until well-risen and golden brown. Do not open the oven door while the Yorkshires are cooking or they may collapse.

Remove from the oven and crumble some haggis into the hollow inside each Yorkshire pudding. Top with a spoonful of red onion chutney and pop back into the oven for 3–4 minutes to warm the filling and make the Yorkshires even crisper and browner. Serve hot with gravy and vegetables.

VARIATIONS
- Use crumbled goat's cheese instead of Cheddar.
- Add some snipped chives or chopped parsley to the batter.
- Top with spicy mango or peach chutney.

HAGGIS MAC 'N' CHEESE

Mac 'n' cheese is comfort food at its very best: warming, creamy and packed with flavour and nutrients. Adding haggis, cauliflower and tomatoes transforms it into a special and satisfying dish that all the family can enjoy. If wished, you can use traditional instead of vegetarian haggis.

SERVES 4
PREP 15 MINUTES
COOK 35–45 MINUTES
+ COOKING THE HAGGIS

200g (7oz) vegetarian haggis
225g (8oz/2¼ cups) macaroni
1 small cauliflower, trimmed and separated into florets
75g (3oz/1/3 cup) butter
50g (2oz/½ cup) plain (all-purpose) flour
500ml (17fl oz/generous 2 cups) milk
1 tsp Dijon mustard
200g (7oz/2 cups) grated Cheddar cheese
150g (5oz) cherry tomatoes, halved
cayenne pepper, for dusting
sea salt and freshly ground black pepper

Preheat the oven to 190°C (170°C fan)/375°F/gas 5.

Cook the haggis according to the instructions on the packet.

At the same time, cook the macaroni in a pan of boiling salted water according to the instructions on the packet.

While the haggis and macaroni are cooking, add the cauliflower to a large pan of water and cook for 6–8 minutes or until just tender but not mushy – the florets should keep their shape. Drain well and pat with kitchen paper (paper towels) to absorb the moisture.

Melt the butter in a pan set over a low heat. Stir in the flour with a wooden spoon and cook for 2–3 minutes, stirring, until you have a smooth paste. Gradually whisk in the milk, a little at a time, beating until it's all added and free of lumps. Bring to the boil, stirring, until it thickens and you have a smooth, glossy sauce. Reduce the heat to low and cook for 2–3 minutes. Remove the pan from the heat and stir in the mustard and most of the cheese. Season to taste with salt and pepper.

Put the macaroni, cauliflower and tomatoes in a large ovenproof dish and crumble the haggis over the top in a single layer. Cover with the sauce and sprinkle with the remaining cheese.

Bake in the preheated oven for 15–20 minutes until piping hot, crisp and golden brown on top. Dust with cayenne pepper and serve immediately.

> **VARIATIONS**
> • Add some shredded spinach or kale.
> • Use broccoli instead of cauliflower.

HAGGIS PIZZA

Pizzas are a great way to use up leftover haggis as you only need a little for each serving. If you're in a hurry, you can cheat and use ready-made pizza bases or even some large flatbreads or wraps rather than making them yourself. Note that vegans can use non-dairy cheese for the topping.

SERVES 4
PREP 30 MINUTES
RISE 1–2 HOURS
COOK 12–15 MINUTES

240ml (8fl oz/1 cup) passata or tomato/pizza sauce
2 bottled roasted red or yellow (bell) peppers, drained and thinly sliced
¼ red onion, very thinly sliced
225g (8oz) vegetarian haggis, crumbled
200g (7oz) mozzarella cheese, thinly sliced
olive oil, for drizzling

PIZZA BASES:
500g (1lb 2oz/5 cups) strong bread flour, plus extra for dusting
1 x 7g (¼oz) sachet fast-action dried yeast
1 tsp sea salt
300ml (½ pint/1¼ cups) warm water

Tip: Instead of making the dough by hand, use a food mixer fitted with a special dough hook.

Make the dough for the pizza bases: put the flour, yeast and salt into a large mixing bowl. Make a hollow in the centre and pour in most of the warm water. Mix to a soft dough, drawing in the flour from the sides of the bowl. If the dough is too dry, add some more warm water.

Knead the ball of dough on a lightly floured work surface for about 10 minutes, or until smooth, silky and elastic. Place in a clean lightly oiled bowl and cover with cling film (plastic wrap). Leave in a warm place for 1–2 hours until well risen and doubled in size.

Preheat the oven to 230°C (210°C fan)/450°F/gas 8.

Knock the dough down with your fist and knead it lightly on a floured work surface. Cut into four equal-sized pieces and roll each one out thinly into a 20cm (8 inch) circle. Place them on one or two baking trays (sheet pans).

Spread the passata or tomato/pizza sauce over the top, leaving a 2cm (1 inch) border around the edge. Cover with the red or yellow peppers and red onion and crumble the haggis over the top. Dot with mozzarella and drizzle with a little olive oil.

Bake in the preheated oven for 12–15 minutes until the pizza bases are crisp and golden and the mozzarella has melted and is turning golden brown.

VARIATIONS
- Use grated mozzarella or even some Cheddar or Swiss cheese.
- Add some sliced mushrooms.
- Non vegetarians can use regular haggis and add some sliced pepperoni.

SNACKS AND SANDWICHES

SPICY HAGGIS SAMOSAS

These spicy samosas make a healthy snack as they are oven-baked rather than deep-fried in oil. You can also serve them as an appetizer with a cooling raita – just stir some diced cucumber and chopped mint into a bowl of chilled plain Greek yoghurt.

MAKES 8 SAMOSAS
PREP 30 MINUTES
COOK 35–40 MINUTES

450g (1lb) sweet potatoes, peeled and cubed
1 tbsp sunflower oil, plus extra for brushing
1 large onion, finely chopped
2 spring onions (scallions), thinly sliced
2 garlic cloves, crushed
1 red chilli, diced
1 tsp grated fresh root ginger
2 tsp nigella (black onion) seeds
1 tbsp curry paste
200g (7oz) baby spinach leaves
2 tbsp water
a small handful of coriander (cilantro), chopped
225g (8oz) haggis
8 sheets of ready-rolled filo (phyllo) pastry
sea salt and freshly ground black pepper
lime pickle and mango chutney, to serve

Preheat the oven to 200°C (180°C fan)/400°F/gas 6.

Cook the sweet potatoes in a pan of boiling water or a steamer for 10 minutes or until just tender – keep checking it to ensure it does not get too soft and mushy. Drain well.

Meanwhile, heat the oil in a saucepan set over a low heat and cook the onion, spring onions and garlic, stirring occasionally, for 6–8 minutes until softened. Add the chilli, ginger and mustard seeds and cook for 2 minutes until the seeds pop and release their aroma. Stir in the curry paste and cook for 1 minute.

Add the spinach and water, then cover the pan for 1–2 minutes until the spinach leaves wilt and turn bright green. Gently stir in the cooked sweet potato and coriander and crumble in the haggis. Check the seasoning, adding salt and pepper if needed. Set aside to cool.

Place one sheet of filo pastry on a clean worktop and brush lightly with oil. Cover with another sheet and brush with oil. Cut lengthways down the middle into two long rectangles.

Put a spoonful of the cooled sweet potato mixture into the top right-hand corner of each strip of pastry. Fold the pastry over the filling at an angle to make a triangle, then keep on folding it over until you get to the bottom of each strip. You should end up with a neat triangular pastry parcel enclosing the filling. Repeat with the remaining sheets of filo pastry and the sweet potato mixture to make eight samosas.

Brush the samosas lightly with oil and place them on a baking tray (sheet pan) lined with baking parchment. Cook in the preheated oven for 20–25 minutes until crisp and golden. Serve with lime pickle and mango chutney.

VARIATIONS
- Substitute frozen peas for the spinach.
- Add some cumin seeds and a pinch of ground turmeric.
- Use white potatoes instead of sweet potatoes.

CHEESY HAGGIS REUBEN BAGELS

A classic deli Reuben is made with corned beef, but we've given it a Scottish twist and used cooked haggis instead. For a veggie version, substitute vegetarian haggis.

SERVES 4
PREP 10 MINUTES
COOK 10 MINUTES

115g (4oz/½ cup) mayonnaise
60ml (2fl oz/¼ cup) tomato ketchup
1 tbsp horseradish relish or sauce
1 tbsp sweet pickle
50g (2oz/¼ cup) unsalted butter, at room temperature
4 bagels, split in half
4 slices of Swiss cheese, e.g. Emmenthal
4 dill pickles, sliced
300g (10oz) haggis, crumbled (or 4 slices of cooked haggis)
4 heaped tbsp sauerkraut
potato crisps (potato chips) and ketchup, to serve

Preheat the oven to 200°C (180°C fan)/400°F/gas 6. Line a baking tray (sheet pan) with baking paper.

In a bowl, mix together the mayonnaise, ketchup, horseradish and sweet pickle.

Melt the butter in a large frying pan (skillet) set over a medium heat. Add the bagels, cut-side down, to the pan and cook for 4–5 minutes, or until golden brown. Remove and place, cut-side up, on the lined baking tray.

Spread the ketchup mayo mixture over the four bagel bases and cover each one with a cheese slice and the dill pickles.

Carefully spoon a layer of cooked haggis over the top or use cooked haggis slices, then cover with the bagel tops.

Bake in the preheated oven for 5 minutes, or until the cheese melts.

Remove from the oven and take off the bagel tops. Place a heaped tablespoon of sauerkraut on top of the haggis and cover with the bagel tops. Serve immediately with potato crisps and ketchup.

Tip: You can buy sauerkraut in cans or jars in most supermarkets.

VARIATIONS
- Use coleslaw instead of sauerkraut.
- Use hot ketchup or add a dash of hot sauce.
- Spread the cut side of the bagel tops with mustard just before serving.

CHEESY BACON AND HAGGIS TOASTIES

Who doesn't like a crisp toastie, oozing with melted cheese? Upgrade your usual toasted cheese sandwich with some protein-rich haggis and tangy chutney for a very special snack.

SERVES 2
PREP 10 MINUTES
COOK 4-6 MINUTES

4 slices of streaky bacon
4 slices of wholemeal or sourdough bread
30g (1oz/2 tbsp) softened butter, plus extra for frying
2 heaped tbsp good-quality mayo
a small handful of rocket (arugula) leaves
150g (5oz) haggis, crumbled
115g (4oz/generous 1 cup) grated Cheddar cheese
2 heaped tbsp caramelized red onion chutney

Fry the bacon in a non-stick frying pan (skillet) set over a medium to high heat until golden brown and crispy on both sides. Remove and drain on kitchen paper (paper towels).

Spread one side only of the bread slices with butter. Take two slices and spread the mayo over the unbuttered sides. Layer the rocket, haggis, cheese and bacon on top and add a spoonful of chutney. Cover with the remaining slices of bread, buttered side outwards, and press down firmly.

Add a little butter to the frying pan and set over a medium heat. When the pan is hot and the butter has melted, add the sandwiches and fry gently for 2–3 minutes on both sides, pressing down gently with a spatula, until they are uniformly golden brown and the cheese has melted.

Remove from the pan and enjoy.

> **VARIATIONS**
> - Add a little extra heat by drizzling with hot sauce.
> - Use sliced ham instead of bacon and add sliced tomatoes.

HAGGIS LOADED POTATO SKINS

If you love crispy loaded potato skins oozing with melted cheese, try these with added vegetarian haggis. They're delicious and very 'more-ish'. If wished, substitute regular haggis for the vegetarian one we've used here.

MAKES 8 POTATO SKINS
PREP 15 MINUTES
COOK 60–70 MINUTES

4 baking potatoes, washed and scrubbed
olive oil, for brushing and frying
8 tbsp Bashed Neeps (mashed swede) (see page 27)
a few sprigs of parsley, chopped
50g (2oz/¼ cup) butter
200g (7oz) vegetarian haggis, crumbled
50g (2oz/½ cup) grated Cheddar cheese
coarse sea salt and freshly ground black pepper

Note: Vegans can make these skins with vegan butter and cheese.

Preheat the oven to 200°C (180°C fan)/400°F/gas 6.

Brush the potatoes with oil and sprinkle with coarse sea salt. Place on a baking tray (sheet pan) and cook in the preheated oven for 50–60 minutes, or until the skins are crisp and the flesh inside soft.

Cut the potatoes in half lengthways and scoop out some of the flesh to leave a hollow in the centre. There should be about 5mm (¼ inch) potato left inside each skin to form a shell.

Heat a little oil in a non-stick frying pan (skillet) set over a medium to high heat and add the potato shells, skin-side down. Cook for 2–3 minutes to crisp them up and then turn them over and fry the top 'rims' of the potato shells for 2 minutes until crispy and golden.

Mix a little of the potato flesh with the swede, parsley and butter, gently mashing them together (keep any leftover potato for another meal). Season to taste with salt and pepper.

Fill the potato shells with the mixture and place on a baking tray. Top with the crumbled haggis and sprinkle with cheese.

Pop back into the hot oven for 6–8 minutes until the cheese has melted and is bubbling and golden brown. Serve hot.

> **VARIATIONS**
> - Add some crumbled crispy bacon or diced ham.
> - Top with a dollop of soured cream or yoghurt and sprinkle with chives.
> - Dust with cayenne or chilli powder.

VEGAN HAGGIS FILO PARCELS

Make these delicious vegan treats with vegan filo (phyllo) pastry (available in most supermarkets and delis). You can enjoy them hot or cold and they will keep well in a sealed container in the fridge for up to 3 days. They can be frozen for up to 3 months.

MAKES 24 PARCELS
PREP 30 MINUTES
COOK 20–25 MINUTES

400g (14oz) swede (rutabaga), peeled and diced
freshly grated nutmeg, to taste
300g (10oz) vegan haggis (see note)
4 sheets of ready-rolled vegan filo (phyllo) pastry
sunflower or light olive oil, for brushing
sea salt and freshly ground black pepper
cranberry sauce or redcurrant jelly, to serve

VARIATIONS
- Use regular haggis and melted butter instead of oil.
- Use leftover Bashed Neeps (swede or turnip) and/or Tatties (see page 27) instead of cooking fresh swede.
- Serve with Whisky Sauce (see page 23).

Preheat the oven to 190°C (170°C fan)/375°F/gas 5. Line a baking tray (sheet pan) with baking parchment.

Cook the swede in a pan of boiling salted water for 10–12 minutes, or until just tender but not mushy – they should still be a little firm and keep their shape. Drain well in a colander and then transfer to a bowl.

Mash the swede coarsely and season to taste with salt and pepper and some grated nutmeg. Crumble the haggis into the bowl and mix everything together.

Place one sheet of filo pastry on a clean work surface and cut in half horizontally. Cut each half sheet lengthways into three strips, so you end up with six long strips.

Put a spoonful of the cooled swede and haggis mixture in the top right-hand corner of each strip of pastry. Fold the pastry over the filling at an angle to make a triangle, then keep on folding it over until you get to the bottom of each strip. You should end up with a neat triangular parcel enclosing the filling. Repeat with the remaining sheets of filo pastry and the swede and haggis mixture to make 24 parcels.

Lightly brush the parcels with oil and place on the lined baking tray. Cook in the preheated oven for 20–25 minutes, or until crisp and golden. Serve warm with cranberry sauce or redcurrant jelly.

Note: Our vegetarian haggis recipe (see page 19) is suitable for vegans, too.

SNACKS AND SANDWICHES

HAGGIS SCOTCH EGGS

These crispy Scotch eggs are perfect for packed lunches, picnics and snacks. They are easy to make and keep well stored in an airtight container in the fridge for up to 3 days.

MAKES 6
PREP 25 MINUTES
COOK 16–20 MINUTES

8 medium free-range eggs, at room temperature
400g (14oz) haggis
200g (7oz) pork sausage meat
plain (all-purpose) flour, for dusting
150g (5oz/1⅓ cups) dried breadcrumbs or panko breadcrumbs
sunflower or vegetable oil, for deep-frying
tomato ketchup or hot sauce, to serve

Tip: For vegetarian Scotch eggs, use the Vegetarian Haggis mixture (see page 19) for moulding around the eggs.

VARIATIONS
- Serve with a spicy or fruity chutney or some piccalilli.
- Use fresh breadcrumbs instead of dried.

Bring a large pan of water to the boil and then lower six of the eggs into the pan. Reduce the heat and simmer for 7 minutes. Remove the eggs with a slotted spoon and plunge them into a bowl of iced water. When they are cool enough to handle, carefully peel away the shells.

Beat one of the eggs in a bowl and mix together with the haggis and sausage meat.

Divide the mixture into six portions and flatten each one into a 20cm (8 inch) round, either with your hands or by rolling it out gently with a rolling pin between two sheets of cling film (plastic wrap).

Place a boiled egg on one of the haggis rounds and, with wet hands, wrap it around the egg, so it is completely covered. Gently mould and squeeze the joins together to seal the egg inside. Repeat with the other eggs and dust gently with flour.

Beat the remaining egg in a bowl. Dip the coated eggs into the beaten egg and then roll them in the breadcrumbs or panko until coated all over.

Pour enough oil into a deep heavy-based saucepan to come halfway up the sides. Place over a medium to high heat and when the temperature reaches 160°C (320°F) (use a sugar thermometer to check), add the Scotch eggs, two or three at a time, depending on the size of the pan. Fry for 8–10 minutes, turning once or twice, until crisp and golden brown all over. Remove carefully with a slotted spoon and drain on kitchen paper (paper towels).

Serve the Scotch eggs, cut in half, with some tomato ketchup or hot sauce.

HAGGIS SAUSAGE ROLLS

Serve these tasty bites as party canapés, with pre-dinner drinks or as a delicious snack. Using ready-made pre-rolled puff pastry takes all the hassle out of making the rolls.

MAKES 20 SAUSAGE ROLLS
PREP 25 MINUTES
COOK 20 MINUTES

300g (10oz) haggis, crumbled
150g (5oz) pork sausage meat
1 small onion, finely chopped
a few sage leaves, finely chopped
320g (10½oz) ready-rolled puff pastry sheet
1 medium free-range egg, beaten
sea salt and freshly ground black pepper

VARIATIONS
- Serve with some ketchup, honey mustard or caramelized red onion chutney.
- Use vegetarian haggis instead of regular haggis and pork sausage meat.
- Sprinkle the rolls with sesame seeds before baking.

Preheat the oven to 220°C (200°C fan)/425°F/gas 7. Line two baking trays (sheet pans) with baking parchment.

Put the haggis and sausage meat in a bowl with the onion and sage. Season lightly with salt and pepper.

Spread the pastry sheet out on a lightly floured work surface and cut it in half lengthways.

Divide the haggis filling into two equal-sized portions and, with your hands, roll each one into a long cylinder, the same length as the strips of pastry.

Lay one cylinder along one long side of each strip of pastry and brush the other long edge with beaten egg. Fold the pastry over the haggis filling and seal the edges together to enclose the filling. Roll the cylinder over with the sealed edge underneath.

Brush each filled cylinder with beaten egg and then cut into 10 sausage rolls. Snip the top of each roll with scissors and place them on the lined baking trays.

Bake in the preheated oven for 20 minutes, or until golden brown and crisp – the haggis sausage meat inside should be cooked through. Transfer to a wire rack to cool, then store in an airtight container in the fridge for up to 3 days.

Tip: If you can't buy sausage meat, just remove some good-quality pork sausages from their skins.

JALAPENO HAGGIS CHEESE SCONES

These delicious cheese scones make great snacks or teatime treats. You can even serve them as a savoury accompaniment to hot vegetable soup.

MAKES ABOUT 18 SCONES
PREP 15 MINUTES
REST 15–20 MINUTES
COOK 12–15 MINUTES

450g (1lb/4 cups) self-raising flour, plus extra for dusting
2 level tsp baking powder
115g (4oz/½ cup) softened butter
225g (8oz/2 cups) grated mature Cheddar cheese
1–2 fresh jalapenos, deseeded and finely chopped
100g (3½oz) haggis, crumbled
2 heaped tsp wholegrain mustard
175ml (6fl oz/¾ cup) milk, plus extra for brushing
2 tsp sesame seeds

Preheat the oven to 200°C (180°C fan)/400°F/gas 6.

Sift the flour and baking powder into a mixing bowl and rub in the butter with your fingertips until it resembles breadcrumbs. Stir in the grated cheese, jalapenos, haggis and mustard. Add sufficient milk to form a workable soft dough, and then turn out onto a lightly floured surface.

Lightly roll out the dough, about 4cm (1½ inches) thick. Cut into rounds with a 5cm (2 inch) cutter and place on a baking tray (sheet pan) and sprinkle with sesame seeds. Set aside to rest for 15–20 minutes.

Lightly brush the tops of the scones with milk and bake near the top of the preheated oven for 12–15 minutes, until risen and golden brown. Cool slightly on a wire rack.

Serve the scones hot or warm. If wished, split them in half and butter generously. They will keep well in an airtight container for up to 3 days

Tip: If the scone mixture seems a bit dry, just add a little more milk to moisten it so it comes together as a soft dough.

VARIATIONS
- Add some snipped chives to the mix.
- Substitute buttermilk for regular milk.
- Use pickled jalapenos if you don't have fresh ones. Otherwise, regular green or red chillies work well.

CHEESY HAGGIS NACHOS

Nachos are so versatile – they make a tasty snack or are the perfect accompaniment to pre-dinner drinks. Plus, they're so quick and easy to make and there's hardly any washing up. We've used traditional haggis, but you can swap it for veggie haggis if you prefer.

SERVES 4
PREP 10 MINUTES
COOK 10 MINUTES

225g (8oz) salted corn tortilla chips
4 ripe tomatoes, deseeded and diced
1 x 400g (14oz) can kidney beans, rinsed and drained
200g (7oz) haggis, crumbled
1 bunch of spring onions (scallions), finely sliced
4 pickled jalapenos, thinly sliced
100g (3½oz/1 cup) grated Cheddar or Monterey Jack cheese
150g (5oz/1 cup) guacamole
150g (5oz/1 cup) hot tomato salsa
soured cream or Greek yoghurt, to serve

Preheat the oven to 200°C (180°C fan)/400°F/gas 6.

Put the tortilla chips in a large ovenproof dish and scatter the tomatoes, kidney beans, crumbled haggis, spring onions and jalapenos over the top. Sprinkle with the grated cheese.

Bake in the preheated oven for 10 minutes or until everything is really hot and the cheese is golden brown, melted and bubbling.

Spoon the guacamole and salsa over the top and serve with soured cream or yoghurt.

VARIATIONS
- Instead of pickled jalapenos, use 2 sliced hot red or green chillies.
- Substitute canned black beans for kidney beans.
- Sprinkle with chopped coriander (cilantro).
- Drizzle with hot sauce.
- Add some diced avocado tossed in lime juice.

HAGGIS BAO BUNS

If you have the time, make the bao buns yourself – they are so delicious and well worth the effort. Alternatively, you can now buy ready-made bao buns in some delis and supermarkets.

MAKES 16 BUNS
PREP 40 MINUTES
RISE 1–2 HOURS
PROVE 30–60 MINUTES
COOK 12–24 MINUTES
+ COOKING THE HAGGIS

400g (14oz) slices of haggis
120ml (4fl oz/½ cup) hoisin sauce
¼ cucumber, sliced or cut into batons
1 bunch of spring onions (scallions), shredded
pickled red onions and carrots
a few sprigs of coriander (cilantro)

BAO BUNS:
240ml (8fl oz/1 cup) warm water (hand-hot: 43–46°C/110–115°F)
3 tbsp sugar
1 tsp active dried yeast
350g (12oz/3½ cups) plain (all-purpose) flour, plus extra for dusting
1½ tsp baking powder
1 tsp salt
85ml (3fl oz/⅓ cup) milk
2 tbsp extra-virgin olive oil

Make the bao buns: put the warm water, 1 tablespoon sugar and yeast in a small bowl and stir well to combine. Set aside for about 5–10 minutes until foamy.

Sift the flour and baking powder into a large bowl. Add the salt and the remaining sugar and mix together. Make a well in the centre and pour in the yeast mixture and the milk together with the oil.

Mix until you have a soft ball of dough – if it's too dry, add a little water. Knead the dough on a floured surface with your hands for 4–5 minutes, or until it's silky smooth and elastic.

Lightly oil a clean bowl and add the dough. Cover with a damp tea towel and leave in a warm place for 1–2 hours, or until it rises.

Place the dough on a floured surface and punch it down with your fists. Cut into 16 equal-sized pieces and place them on a sheet of baking parchment. Roll them out to 1cm (½ inch) thickness and brush lightly with oil before folding the circles over in half (to make a semi-circle) and pressing down gently on top so they stick together. Cover with a damp tea towel or cling film (plastic wrap) and set aside for 30–60 minutes, until puffy.

When you're ready to cook the buns, line a steamer with baking parchment and set it over a pan of boiling water (about 5cm/2 inches of water). Steam the buns in batches, leaving some space in between them, for 6–8 minutes, or until risen and set. Check the water from time to time to make sure the pan doesn't get dry.

Cook the haggis according to the instructions on the packet. Split the steamed buns open and divide the haggis among them. Drizzle with hoisin sauce and add the cucumber, spring onions and pickled vegetables. Sprinkle with coriander and enjoy while the buns are still hot.

SNACKS AND SANDWICHES

INDEX

A
Africa 8
air fryers 11
apples
  haggis sausages with red cabbage 70
Australia 8
avocados
  haggis burrito night dinner 72
  smashed avocado 54
  spicy haggis tacos 62

B
bacon
  Balmoral chicken 32
  cheesy bacon and haggis toasties 97
  creamy haggis soup 42
  the full Scottish 64
  haggis pigs in blankets 40
  haggis sushi 43
bagels, cheesy haggis Reuben 96
baked haggis stuffed vegetables 60
Balmoral chicken 32
banh mi, veggie haggis 52
bao buns, haggis 107
barley
  vegetarian/vegan haggis 18–19
bashed neeps 27
  haggis bubble and squeak patties 30
  haggis loaded potato skins 98
  haggis stacks with whisky sauce 28–9
beans
  cheesy haggis nachos 106
  haggis burrito night dinner 72
  haggis chilli salsa pot 75
  spicy haggis tacos 62
beef
  cheesy haggis baked potatoes 58
  easy reduced-fat haggis 17
  haggis cheeseburgers 82
  haggis chilli salsa pot 75

haggis lasagne 86
haggis meatballs and spaghetti 84–5
homemade traditional haggis 15
bell peppers *see* peppers (bell)
black beans
  haggis burrito night dinner 72
  spicy haggis tacos 62
bread
  cheesy bacon and haggis toasties 97
  haggis pitta pockets with tzatziki 59
  veggie haggis banh mi 52
breadcrumbs
  haggis chicken Kiev 71
  haggis Scotch eggs 102
Brussels sprouts
  haggis bubble and squeak patties 30
bubble and squeak patties 30
buns, bao 107
burgers
  haggis cheeseburgers 82
Burns, Robert 7
  Address to a Haggis 7, 9
Burns Night 7, 9
Burns Night supper 25–33
  Balmoral chicken 32
  haggis bubble and squeak patties 30
  haggis hash and eggs 31
  haggis stacks with whisky sauce 28–9
  haggis with tatties and neeps 26–7
burrito night dinner 72
butter, garlic 71

C
cabbage
  haggis sausages with red cabbage 70
  steamed Chinese haggis dumplings 36–7
Canada 8
caramelized onion gravy 78
carrots
  cheesy haggis baked potatoes 58

haggis hash and eggs 31
haggis hotpot 74
haggis shepherd's pie 83
ragu sauce 86
vegetarian/vegan haggis 18–19
veggie haggis banh mi 52
cauliflower
  haggis mac 'n' cheese 90
cheese
  cheesy bacon and haggis toasties 97
  cheesy haggis baked potatoes 58
  cheesy haggis, mushroom and spinach quesadillas 54
  cheesy haggis nachos 106
  cheesy haggis Reuben bagels 96
  cheesy haggis Yorkshires 88
  cheesy leek and neeps haggis tart 50–1
  festive cheesy haggis bites 39
  the full Scottish 64
  haggis burrito night dinner 72
  haggis cheeseburgers 82
  haggis croquettes 38
  haggis lasagne 86
  haggis loaded potato skins 98
  haggis mac 'n' cheese 90
  haggis meatballs and spaghetti 84–5
  haggis pitta pockets with tzatziki 59
  haggis pizza 91
  haggis Portobello mushrooms with chèvre 48
  haggis shepherd's pie 83
  jalapeno haggis cheese scones 105
  veggie haggis balls with rice 63
chicken
  Balmoral chicken 32
  haggis chicken Kiev 71
  haggis hotpot 74
  roast chicken with haggis stuffing 87
chicken livers
  easy reduced-fat haggis 17
chickpeas (garbanzos)

INDEX

vegan haggis curry 79
chilli powder
   chilli haggis 52
   haggis chilli salsa pot 75
chillies
   cheesy haggis, mushroom and spinach quesadillas 54
   haggis kofta kebabs 55
   jalapeno haggis cheese scones 105
   pico de gallo 72
   spicy haggis samosas 94–5
   spicy tomato salsa 75
   tomato chilli jam 38
   vegan haggis curry 79
Chinese haggis dumplings 36–7
cilantro *see* coriander
cooking techniques 11
coriander (cilantro)
   pico de gallo 72
   spicy haggis samosas 94–5
   spicy tomato salsa 75
   vegan haggis curry 79
cream
   cheesy leek and neeps haggis tart 50–1
   whisky sauce 23
creamy haggis soup 42
croquettes, haggis 38
cucumber
   haggis bao buns 107
   haggis pitta pockets with tzatziki 59
   haggis sushi 43
   tzatziki 59
   veggie haggis banh mi 52
curry
   spicy haggis samosas 94–5
   vegan haggis curry 79

D
dietary fibre 10
dipping sauce 36–7

dumplings, steamed Chinese haggis 36–7

E
easy haggis and mushroom plait 46
easy-peasy tomato sauce 63
easy reduced-fat haggis 17
eggs
   the full Scottish 64
   haggis hash and eggs 31
   haggis Scotch eggs 102
   veggie haggis, neeps and spinach frittata 56
England 9
Europe 8

F
Far East 8
festive cheesy haggis bites 39
fibre, dietary 10
filo (phyllo) pastry
   haggis, swede and spinach filo pie 80
   spicy haggis samosas 94–5
   vegan haggis filo parcels 100
food labels 10
frittata
   veggie haggis, neeps and spinach frittata 56
the full Scottish 64

G
garbanzos *see* chickpeas
garlic
   garlic butter 71
   haggis chilli salsa pot 75
   marinara sauce 84–5
glaze, sticky 49
goat's cheese
   haggis Portobello mushrooms with chèvre 48
gravy
   caramelized onion gravy 78

   mushroom gravy 20
   onion gravy 21
   whisky gravy 22
Greece 9
guacamole
   cheesy haggis nachos 106

H
haggis 8
   cooking 11
   health benefits 10
   name 9
   origins 9
haggis and garlicky spring onion mash 78
haggis bao buns 107
haggis bubble and squeak patties 30
haggis burrito night dinner 72
haggis cheeseburgers 82
haggis chicken Kiev 71
haggis chilli salsa pot 75
haggis croquettes with tomato chilli jam 38
haggis hash and eggs 31
haggis hotpot 74
haggis kofta kebabs 55
haggis lasagne 86
haggis loaded potato skins 98
haggis mac 'n' cheese 90
haggis meatballs and spaghetti 84–5
haggis pigs in blankets 40
haggis pitta pockets with tzatziki 59
haggis pizza 91
haggis Portobello mushrooms with chèvre 48
haggis sausage rolls 103
haggis sausages 16
haggis sausages with red cabbage 70
haggis Scotch eggs 102
haggis shepherd's pie 83
haggis stacks with whisky sauce 28–9
haggis sushi 43
haggis, swede and spinach filo pie 80

INDEX

haggis toad in the hole 76
haggis Wellington 68
haggis with tatties and neeps 26–7
health benefits 10
heart, lamb's
   homemade traditional haggis 15
history of haggis 9
Hogmanay 8
hoisin sauce
   haggis bao buns 107
homemade traditional haggis 15
Homer, *The Odyssey* 9
honey
   sticky glaze 49
hotdogs, sticky haggis 49
hotpot, haggis 74

I
Iceland 9
iron 10

J
jalapeno peppers
   cheesy haggis nachos 106
   jalapeno haggis cheese scones 105

K
kale
   haggis stacks with whisky sauce 28–9
kebabs, haggis kofta 55
ketchup
   cheesy haggis Reuben bagels 96
   sticky glaze 49
kidney beans
   cheesy haggis nachos 106
   haggis chilli salsa pot 75

L
lamb
   haggis kofta kebabs 55
   homemade traditional haggis 15

Lancashire 9
lasagne, haggis 86
leeks
   cheesy leek and neeps haggis tart 50–1
   creamy haggis soup 42
   haggis hotpot 74
   vegan haggis curry 79
lettuce
   haggis burrito night dinner 72
   haggis cheeseburgers 82
liver 10
   easy reduced-fat haggis 17
lungs, sheep's 8, 10

M
macaroni
   haggis mac 'n' cheese 90
marinara sauce 84–5
Marmite
   vegetarian/vegan haggis 18–19
Marsala
   mushroom sauce 32
mayonnaise
   cheesy haggis Reuben bagels 96
   haggis cheeseburgers 82
   spicy mayo 52
meatballs
   haggis meatballs and spaghetti 84–5
microwave ovens 11
minerals 10
mushrooms
   cheesy haggis, mushroom and spinach quesadillas 54
   easy haggis and mushroom plait 46
   the full Scottish 64
   haggis Portobello mushrooms with chèvre 48
   haggis Wellington 68
   mushroom gravy 20
   mushroom sauce 32
   vegetarian/vegan haggis 18–19

N
nachos, cheesy haggis 106
neeps *see* swede (rutabaga)
New Zealand 8
Norfolk 9
nori seaweed
   haggis sushi 43

O
oatmeal
   easy reduced-fat haggis 17
   homemade traditional haggis 15
   vegetarian/vegan haggis 18–19
The Odyssey (Homer) 9
olives
   haggis pitta pockets with tzatziki 59
onions
   baked haggis stuffed vegetables 60
   caramelized onion gravy 78
   cheesy leek and neeps haggis tart 50–1
   easy haggis and mushroom plait 46
   easy reduced-fat haggis 17
   haggis bubble and squeak patties 30
   haggis hotpot 74
   haggis shepherd's pie 83
   haggis, swede and spinach filo pie 80
   onion gravy 21
   pico de gallo 72
   vegan haggis curry 79
   see also spring onions
oranges
   haggis sausages with red cabbage 70
oven baking 11

P
parsnips
   haggis hash and eggs 31
   vegetarian/vegan haggis 18–19
pasta
   haggis lasagne 86
   haggis mac 'n' cheese 90

INDEX

haggis meatballs and spaghetti 84–5
pastries
   easy haggis and mushroom plait 46
   festive cheesy haggis bites 39
   haggis sausage rolls 103
   haggis, swede and spinach filo pie 80
   haggis Wellington 68
   spicy haggis samosas 94–5
   vegan haggis filo parcels 100
pastry, shortcrust 50–1
patties, haggis bubble and squeak 30
pearl barley
   vegetarian/vegan haggis 18–19
peppers (bell)
   baked haggis stuffed vegetables 60
   haggis chilli salsa pot 75
   haggis pizza 91
   veggie haggis banh mi 52
   veggie haggis, neeps and spinach frittata 56
phyllo pastry *see* filo pastry
pico de gallo 72
pigs in blankets 40
pitta breads
   haggis pitta pockets with tzatziki 59
pizza, haggis 91
pork *see* sausage meat
potatoes
   cheesy haggis baked potatoes 58
   haggis and garlicky spring onion mash 78
   haggis bubble and squeak patties 30
   haggis croquettes 38
   haggis hash and eggs 31
   haggis hotpot 74
   haggis loaded potato skins 98
   haggis shepherd's pie 83
   haggis stacks with whisky sauce 28–9
   haggis with tatties and neeps 26–7
   roast chicken with haggis stuffing 87
protein 10

Q
quesadillas
   cheesy haggis, mushroom and spinach quesadillas 54

R
radishes
   veggie haggis banh mi 52
ragu sauce 86
red cabbage, haggis sausages with 70
reduced-fat haggis 17
Reuben bagels, cheesy haggis 96
rice
   baked haggis stuffed vegetables 60
   haggis burrito night dinner 72
   haggis sushi 43
   veggie haggis balls with rice 63
rutabaga *see* swede

S
St Andrew's Day 8
salsa, spicy tomato 75
samosas, spicy haggis 94–5
sauces
   caramelized onion gravy 78
   dipping sauce 36–7
   easy-peasy tomato sauce 63
   marinara sauce 84–5
   mushroom gravy 20
   mushroom sauce 32
   onion gravy 21
   ragu sauce 86
   whisky gravy 22
   whisky sauce 23
   white sauce 86
sauerkraut
   cheesy haggis Reuben bagels 96
sausage meat
   haggis sausage rolls 103
   haggis sausages 16
   haggis Scotch eggs 102
sausages
   haggis and garlicky spring onion mash 78
   haggis pigs in blankets 40
   haggis sausages 16
   haggis sausages with red cabbage 70
   haggis toad in the hole 76
   sticky haggis hotdogs 49
scallions *see* spring onions
Scandinavia 9
scones
   jalapeno haggis cheese scones 105
Scotch eggs, haggis 102
seaweed
   haggis sushi 43
selenium 10
shepherd's pie 83
shortcrust pastry 50–1
soup, creamy haggis 42
soured cream
   haggis burrito night dinner 72
soy sauce
   dipping sauce 36–7
spaghetti
   haggis meatballs and spaghetti 84–5
spicy haggis samosas 94–5
spicy haggis tacos 62
spicy mayo 52
spicy tomato salsa 75
spinach
   cheesy haggis, mushroom and spinach quesadillas 54
   the full Scottish 64
   haggis, swede and spinach filo pie 80
   spicy haggis samosas 94–5
   veggie haggis, neeps and spinach frittata 56
split peas
   vegetarian/vegan haggis 18–19
spring onions (scallions)
   cheesy haggis, mushroom and spinach quesadillas 54
   cheesy haggis nachos 106

INDEX

haggis bao buns 107
haggis and garlicky spring onion mash 78
spicy haggis samosas 94–5
spicy mayo 52
steamed Chinese haggis dumplings 36–7
stews
  haggis hotpot 74
sticky haggis hotdogs 49
stomach, sheep's
  homemade traditional haggis 15
stuffing, haggis 87
sushi, haggis 43
swede (rutabaga)
  cheesy leek and neeps haggis tart 50–1
  creamy haggis soup 42
  haggis bubble and squeak patties 30
  haggis hash and eggs 31
  haggis loaded potato skins 98
  haggis shepherd's pie 83
  haggis stacks with whisky sauce 28–9
  haggis, swede and spinach filo pie 80
  haggis with tatties and neeps 26–7
  roast chicken with haggis stuffing 87
  vegan haggis filo parcels 100
  veggie haggis, neeps and spinach frittata 56
Sweden 9
sweet potatoes
  spicy haggis samosas 94–5

T
tacos, spicy haggis 62
tart, cheesy leek and neeps haggis 50–1
tatties *see* potatoes
toad in the hole 76
toasties, cheesy bacon and haggis 97
tomato ketchup
  cheesy haggis Reuben bagels 96
  sticky glaze 49
tomatoes
  baked haggis stuffed vegetables 60
  cheesy haggis nachos 106

easy-peasy tomato sauce 63
the full Scottish 64
haggis cheeseburgers 82
haggis chilli salsa pot 75
haggis mac 'n' cheese 90
haggis pitta pockets with tzatziki 59
haggis pizza 91
marinara sauce 84–5
pico de gallo 72
ragu sauce 86
spicy haggis tacos 62
spicy tomato salsa 75
tomato chilli jam 38
vegan haggis curry 79
tortilla chips
  cheesy haggis nachos 106
tortillas
  haggis burrito night dinner 72
  cheesy haggis, mushroom and spinach quesadillas 54
tzatziki 59

U
United States of America 8

V
vegan haggis 8, 10, 18–19
  vegan haggis curry 79
  vegan haggis filo parcels 100
vegetarian haggis 8, 10, 18–19
  baked haggis stuffed vegetables 60
  cheesy haggis, mushroom and spinach quesadillas 54
  cheesy leek and neeps haggis tart 50–1
  easy haggis and mushroom plait 46
  festive cheesy haggis bites 39
  haggis burrito night dinner 72
  haggis croquettes with tomato chilli jam 38
  haggis loaded potato skins 98
  haggis mac 'n' cheese 90
  haggis pitta pockets with tzatziki 59

haggis pizza 91
haggis Portobello mushrooms with chèvre 48
haggis sushi 43
haggis, swede and spinach filo pie 80
spicy haggis tacos 62
veggie haggis balls with rice 63
veggie haggis banh mi 52
veggie haggis, neeps and spinach frittata 56
vitamins 10

W
water, cooking in 11
whisky
  whisky gravy 22
  whisky sauce 23
  haggis stacks with whisky sauce 28–9
white sauce 86
wine
  haggis hotpot 74
  mushroom sauce 32
wrappers, dumpling 36–7

Y
yellow split peas
  vegetarian/vegan haggis 18–19
yoghurt
  tzatziki 59
  vegan haggis curry 79
Yorkshires, cheesy haggis 88

Z
zinc 10